"This is a beautiful and tender book that would touch any woman's heart, no matter her age or realm of experience. It is about a relationship so intimate with God that it carves a safe place for crises of faith, for faith proved genuine, and for divine callings willed, sealed, and fulfilled. Yes, this is one mother's moving story. This one mother also happens to be a true writer. We will hear more from her. Angie, I am so proud of you. May Christ continue to tip the ink jar toward your gifted quill."
—Beth Moore, best-selling author and speaker

I Will Carry You

The Sacred Dance of Grief and Joy

Angie Smith

B&H
PUBLISHING GROUP

978-0-8054-6428-3

Published by B&H Publishing Group
Nashville, Tennessee

Dewey Decimal Classification: 155.9
Subject Heading: JOY AND SORROW \
GRACE \ INFANTS—DEATH

Unless otherwise noted, all Scripture quotations are
taken from the *New International Version* copyright ©
1973, 1978, 1984 International Bible Society. Used by permission of Zondervan. All rights reserved. Other versions include
the New American Standard Bible, NASB,
© the Lockman Foundation, 1960, 1962, 1963, 1968, 1971,
1972, 1973, 1975, 1977, 1995; used by permission.

1 2 3 4 5 6 7 8 • 14 13 12 11 10

Contents

For her…

For Him.

Chapter 1
Us

And the cup he brings, though it burn your lips,
has been fashioned of the clay which the Potter
has moistened with His own sacred tears.
—Kahlil Gibran*

If there is one thing I have learned about raising three daughters, it is this: it is an unspoken law that if you are running late, you will not be able to find the sixth shoe.

It's life as a mommy. They are running in every direction, full of life: and all the while you are trying to rein them in and explain why Mrs. Adams won't understand if we are late for gymnastics again. Most of the time I just giggled and chased them around until I inevitably caved and let them wear mismatched shoes, imagining the looks of horror I would receive from the on-time moms.

Our biggest problems in life during the girls' younger years were things like finding the sixth shoe.

---

* I have been encouraged and ministered to by the words of various writers as I've gone through the grieving process. I am so thankful for the way the Lord has used their words in my life. However, quoting specific words from any author should not be understood to be an endorsement or sign of agreement with everything they have written.

I miss those days.

We made plans for forever, like you're supposed to do when you're a family. We were so in love with our life that it was impossible to consider anything else. Just love one another deeply and try to make each moment count for something. Run the race with joy, and it will all be OK.

How could we have known?

And even if we had, I can't say we would have done it any differently. We loved without abandon, each day and night filled with the hope and expectation that we would always be together. Whether nestled under a cozy quilt watching a movie or photographing the girls having a hose fight with the neighbor kids in the backyard, one thing was for sure . . .

We were a family, and everything was exactly as it should be.

My husband Todd sings in a Christian group called Selah, and when I look back at the way God started our family, I can't help but wonder how we managed to keep our sanity.

Just a few months after we were married, I was right in the middle of a conversation with Todd when it happened. I don't remember what we were talking about, but I do know I made a rather abrupt exit as I dashed to the bathroom with my hand over my mouth. I spent the next few hours assuming I had a nasty flu, but in the morning I realized the timing of this "flu" was a little suspicious. Todd ran to the store and bought our first of many pregnancy tests, and I watched as the little line told me I was going to be a mommy. We were completely shocked, but after about six more tests (anyone else done this?) with the same result, I figured it was really happening. I stared in the mirror as I got ready to go out that day, looking at my reflection and imagining what it was going to look like in the coming days.

I never got the chance to see that.

At around nine weeks I miscarried the baby, and I was devastated. Todd was sad, but he hadn't connected the way I had with the baby. His biggest concern was making sure I was OK. He was so tender with me as I tried to process the fact that there had been a life inside me that was gone.

That was the first time in our marriage that we had to walk through loss. We knew it wouldn't be our last, and that our vows included times like these, but it was hard. As a woman, I wondered if something was wrong with me. I would stay awake at night and wonder if I would ever have children. I had just finished a graduate degree in developmental psychology, and pretty much every decision I had made in my life revolved around my love for children. I couldn't help but wonder if motherhood wasn't going to happen the way I had always dreamed it would.

We were fortunate that the Lord didn't wait long to bless us again. I will never forget being out on the road with Todd, sensing that something was happening. It was eleven at night and I told him we needed to find a store that was open so I could take a pregnancy test. He covered his head with a pillow and laughed (mostly because I said this every month in the hopes that it would come up with the pretty pink line).

"Todd. We're in Maryland. You know how I am with finding my way around. What if I get lost?" He looked up at me with tired eyes, pleading with me to let it go.

"Honey, can we go in the morning? Let's get some sleep, and we can do it on the way out."

Clearly he did not understand the urgency of a woman in this mind-set.

"No, I can't wait. I have got to go now. There has to be something right around the corner." I grabbed the rental car keys and kissed him on the forehead.

He fell back on to the bed, knowing I wasn't going to budge.

"And Toddy? You are seriously going to regret not going with me if it turns out I'm pregnant." I smiled mischievously and closed the door behind me while he laughed.

I came back into the hotel room about a half hour later and ran straight for the bathroom. I watched as the colors changed immediately, clue number one to what we would later discover. Without even bothering to wait for it to make it all the way across the little screen, I opened the bathroom door and held the stick straight in front of me. I waited a second to make sure he was paying attention and then peeked my head out with a giant smile.

Todd sat straight up in bed, his eyes adjusting to the light and his mind adjusting to what was happening.

"Are you serious?"

I nodded.

I screamed with delight and jumped into bed, settling into my familiar spot on his chest.

He grabbed the test and stared at his future.

"Congratulations, Daddy."

In disbelief he set his hands on my stomach.

"Wow." It was about all he could manage.

"Yeah, wow."

We lay in silence for a few minutes, smiling in the darkness.

"Hey babe?" I asked.

"Yeah?"

"You totally should have come with me."

We laughed as we pulled the covers up, both of us in awe that God had chosen us.

And boy, had He ever.

After my initial miscarriage I had gone to the library down the street and checked out a book about pregnancy loss. The sweet librarian recognized me and acknowledged my pain as she scanned the book.

"God bless you, honey." She looked deep into my red eyes, ministering to me without another word.

I started to cry because it was such a simple gesture, and it meant more to me than I knew how to say to her.

After I got the positive test result, I was eager to go back and check out another book—this time, one on pregnancy. I saw the librarian working at the counter and waved. A few minutes later I set down three pregnancy books on the counter, and she clapped her hands in delight.

A few days later I went in for my twelve-week checkup, and they did an ultrasound.

After a rather shocking appointment, I made my way back to the library and smiled when I saw my library friend working. I watched her face light up as I set down a new set of books.

This time they were on parenting *twins*.

She looked up at me in total shock and started laughing.

"Oh, God bless you, honey! I'm sort of hopin' for your sake that I won't be seein' you tomorrow!"

Aside from some discomfort, everything seemed to be going smoothly with my pregnancy, but my doctor suggested I have another ultrasound at around twenty-five weeks just to make sure. We knew we were having two girls and we were pretty set on names. At the end of August, we went in to have another look at the babies, and within about a minute we knew something was terribly wrong. The technician who was doing the ultrasound looked like he was in shock, and he got tears in his eyes as he told us he needed to get his supervisor. I felt like I couldn't breathe, and I asked him if they were alive.

"They are alive right now."

Those words will haunt me for the rest of my life.

His supervisor explained that I was dilated about three and a half centimeters, and that my body was threatening to go into labor. She told me I needed to get right to the hospital, and they called for a wheelchair as they weren't even comfortable with letting me stand up.

I sobbed the whole way over. My first night in the hospital a sweet nurse came in and sat with me, explaining that my babies were on "the cusp of viability," and that they were going to do everything they could to keep them inside me for as many weeks as possible. She was incredibly kind but also honest, and the truth was that it was an incredibly serious and unpredictable situation. A few days later I had surgery to try to prevent my cervix from opening any more. I continued to be on a round of the most horrific drugs known to man.

If you are familiar with magnesium sulfate, you understand. They had me on that one for three weeks. At one point I thought my IV pole was a trick-or-treater. Todd was on the road, and my best friend Audra was with me, so at that point she told me she thought it would be a good idea to go to sleep.

After ten weeks of touch-and-go in the hospital, they felt I was in a safe zone and sent me home. They stopped one of my medications a few days later, and I started having contractions. I had a gloriously short and easy delivery, and on December 2, 2002, we welcomed Ellie and Abby into the world just two minutes apart. Weighing in at four pounds eleven ounces and three pounds eleven ounces respectively, they were tiny but perfect.

Abby was rushed to the NICU immediately, and we never heard her make a sound. She had a few complications with her breathing, but overall she did great. She was an itty-bitty thing, but she was a fighter!

We brought Ellie home from the hospital, set down her baby carrier, and I kissed Todd good-bye as he left for his Christmas tour. I will never forget those first few moments of silence after the door closed behind him. I stared at Ellie in her car seat and just began to weep. I was hormonal, alone, and in charge of two people's lives. I was scared stiff. I had one baby at home and the other in the NICU, and trying to nurse two babies on different schedules who were a half an hour away from each other was, to say the least, very difficult.

One night, when I felt like I had reached the end of myself, I walked into the NICU and heard a familiar sound. It took me a minute to put it together, and when I did, I asked what they were listening to. The nurse (who had no idea who my husband was) replied, "It's the new Selah Christmas CD, and it is so, so great."

I couldn't believe it.

"Do you listen to it a lot?" I asked.

Tears filled my eyes as I anticipated her answer.

"Oh yes, all the time. The babies love it."

I started crying because all this time, when I felt awful that Todd and I couldn't be there with her every moment, God had provided a way for her daddy to be singing over her. The nurses came to me and put their arms around me as I told them who I was and why this CD was so special to me. I remember one of the ladies reminding me that His ways are not our ways and we must believe even when we can't see the way out.

Abby made such great strides that our prayers were answered, and she came home just before Christmas. The high-risk doctor who treated me came into my room one day and, in a hushed tone, told me that my God had performed a miracle. He smiled as he left the room, and at that moment I had no idea that I would see him again a few years down the road in a much different situation.

Lights strung, presents wrapped, and two redheaded bundles that had defied the odds. Could life get any better? In the midst of it all, Todd and I fell in love with each other in a whole new way. We stayed up late at night and played cards in bed, covering each other's mouths to stifle laughter that might wake the babies. We realized the awesome responsibility we had been given and dove into it headfirst.

The peace of God settled into our tiny apartment every night as Todd sang lullabies and I gently rocked the girls to sleep. After sneaking out of their room (which was a closet!), we would play rock-paper-scissors to see who would feed which baby during the night.

The loser had to take Abby, who was notorious for waking up at least ten times during the night. When I would hear her stirring at 4:00 a.m., I would tickle Todd tauntingly and whisper, *"Your baby's up, hon. Have fun!"* He would roll over and whack me with a pillow. The next night we reversed roles. When I think about that time in our lives, I just remember laughter. I really understood what love was supposed to be and who I wanted to be as a mother. We were sleep deprived for sure, but we couldn't get enough of them. We lived in a hazy blur of joy and chaos, knowing that above all we were really in it together now.

A few months later I was dancing with Todd at a friend's wedding, his scruffy cheek pressed against mine as we swayed together in an unspoken promise: *This will never be taken from us.*

We came home from the wedding and ran up to see our sleeping beauties, sweaty headed and flushed with the joy of another full day. Their personalities were starting to take shape, and since we loved Louis Armstrong's "What a Wonderful World," we dubbed the pensive Ellie our "dark sacred night," and gregarious Abby our "bright blessed day." I tucked them deep into the safety of their covers, and the same implicit promise filled the room: *This will always be ours.*

What a wonderful world indeed.

What can I say? The twins were pretty much the perfect kids. They slept all the time, they ate whatever we fed them, they were even tempered, they smiled at strangers, and loved to snuggle. They were the kind of kids people fall in love with the moment they meet them. They wanted to help with everything around the house, cleaned up after themselves, played nicely with all their little friends, and constantly filled the house with the sound of joy.

I began to formulate a theory in my mind, which was based almost entirely on the fact that I must be the most perfect mother to ever grace the face of the earth. I smiled as people marveled at them sitting in the grocery carts while I shopped, and inwardly shook my head as we passed women with their unruly children. I nodded like royalty as women commented that they had never seen such well-behaved, sweet children. *Oh, why thank you. Really? Well, I guess we are just blessed to have such good girls. . . . You are too kind. . . . Oh, how sweet. . . .*

I have an image of God sitting in heaven, munching on a big bowl of popcorn as the days counted down to September 7, 2005.

It was a perfectly planned (see where this is going?), crisp, fall afternoon when Sarah Katherine Smith came raging into the world about an hour and a half after I went into labor (yes, you read that correctly). She screamed like a wild animal in pain when they bathed her, smacked her way out of her newborn blanket, and stared at me with a look that said, "I'm going to need some more information here, lady." I heard a nurse make a comment under her breath about how I was going to have my hands full. I was not at all intimidated.

Clearly, I thought, *they did not know they were dealing with super mom.*

A few months passed, and I realized that the Lord, in His infinite (and often humorous) wisdom, had decided to give me the childhood version of myself to parent. I must say that the level of glowing satisfaction I have seen on my father's face in the past four years has approached sinful.

Kate is the most life-filled, passionate, willful blessing I have ever had the pleasure of raising. We always prayed that we would have a third child who wouldn't slip into the background and be overshadowed by the twins. When I was pregnant with her, I had horrible images of her sitting alone in the corner and feeling like a loner because she didn't have a partner the way they did. We prayed for her to have a voice, to have courage, to have strength, unwavering enthusiasm, determination, and conviction. In retrospect I think we may have overdone it a little.

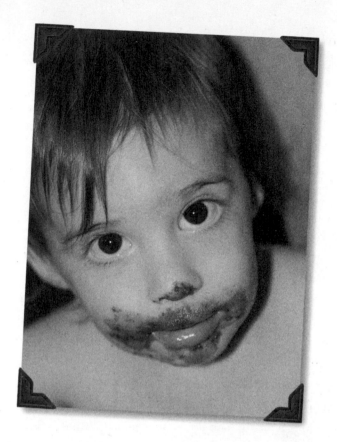

Her enormous brown eyes and deep husky voice bring life into every room she enters. I see a lot of myself in her. You can't keep that girl from what she wants; one day, when she gets her arms around Jesus, she is going to take the world by storm. Until that day, I am drinking a lot of soothing tea and praying that I enter my late thirties with most of my hair.

When Kate was about two, we started talking about having another baby.

Let me restate that.

We had half a conversation and the stick turned pink.

Even from the beginning there was no question that this baby was supposed to be ours. We broke the news to the girls, who proceeded to request a boy who would not be interested in their toys. We told them we would do the best we could.

At about sixteen weeks we went in for a regular ultrasound, and we discovered that we were, much to the girl's chagrin, going to have another pair of sweet little girl hands digging in the Barbie bin. Other than that it was a normal ultrasound, although we did find out later that the technician had noted that there was less fluid than would be expected.

They suggested I have a follow-up ultrasound at around eighteen weeks just to make sure everything looked OK. We headed home with the thought that everything seemed to be all right. I had felt uneasy about this pregnancy from the beginning so it was nice to have a little reassurance. After my experience with Abby and Ellie, it was hard to ever feel totally at peace about being pregnant, but this was different. I felt so uneasy that I had trouble sleeping, and I Googled myself into every possible tragedy.

The kids actually took the gender announcement surprisingly well, and we moved into full swing nesting mode as a family. We took out one of the old cribs and set it up in Kate's room, which she was very pleased about because it meant graduation to a big-girl bed. We talked about names and all the fun things we were going to do with the new baby, and we stared at her ultrasound picture and dreamed of what life would be like with another car seat.

We decided to name her Audrey Caroline after my best friend Audra, with her middle name coming from mine (Carole). The girls were disappointed that we had eliminated "Shimmer," "Rainbow Flurry," and "Feather Dancer" so quickly. Thankfully they approved of Audrey, so it was agreed.

We were going to have another stocking hanging from the mantle next year.

One of my tests came back slightly abnormal, but my doctor wasn't worried because this particular test has an extremely high rate of false positives. He did suggest that I go ahead and have a follow-up ultrasound to see if the baby had Down syndrome. As someone who has worked with this population of children, I wasn't intimidated by the possibility of a special-needs child, but I did want to know so that I could start preparing the children and making every effort to make sure Todd and I were educated.

I was a little nervous about the ultrasound, because as mothers we can't help but imagine the worst-case scenario. I tried to keep myself calm, reminding myself that the Lord had our best interest in mind. He knew what we could handle, and we had to have faith in that. Still, I was uneasy about the appointment; I feared it was more serious than we were anticipating.

My mother-in-law was in town and sensed the Lord told her to stay with me for my appointment so she canceled her flight and decided to come with us. As we sat in the waiting room, we tried to make small talk, but we were so distracted. Something just wasn't right, and we knew it. A nurse emerged abruptly from the door behind us.

"Angie Smith." My stomach jumped.

"We'll be right back, Mom." I looked into the depths of her eyes, and I thought I saw a glimpse of fear.

"Everything will be fine," she said softly.

I kissed her cheek.

"Praying for you, hon." She squeezed my hand, and Todd and I disappeared into the corridors that now hold the worst memories of my life.

The enemy pursues me,
he crushes me to the ground;
he makes me dwell in darkness
like those long dead.
So my spirit grows faint within me;
my heart within me is dismayed.
Psalm 143:3–4

Yet I am always with you;
you hold me by my right hand.
You guide me with your counsel,
and afterward you will take me into glory.
Whom have I in heaven but you?
And earth has nothing I desire besides you.
My flesh and my heart may fail,
but God is the strength of my heart
and my portion forever.
Psalm 73:23–26

Chapter 2
The One You Love

Faith is to believe what we do not see;
the reward of this faith is to see what we believe.
—Saint Augustine

It took the first technician about five minutes to determine that there was a serious problem. I remember her asking me a few yes or no questions, but for the most part she was silent. I kept thinking about how people say, "It felt like a dream—" and suddenly it made sense to me. It really didn't feel like this could be happening to us; after all, we were such a normal family. Things like this just don't happen to people like us, right?

At one point I asked her if the baby was going to live. I was waiting for a yes. Praying for a glimpse of hope.

She shook her head.

"I don't know. There are a lot of issues. I need to get the doctor . . . she seems to be . . . I don't know . . ." she trailed off, took the wand off my stomach and walked out of the room.

I fell into Todd's lap and begged him to tell me it wasn't happening.

Not again.

The room refused to stand still, and I swam in the panic that filled it.

I asked Todd to go get his mother.

Right after he left, Dr. J came in. He looked me in the eye and set his hand gently on my knee. He had an expression that unfortunately I'm sure he had worn many times before. It is the look a doctor has when he is about to tell a tearful mommy that her baby is going to die and nothing can be done about it. He paused for a moment before speaking, and then he began what was to be the longest thirty minutes I had ever experienced. He had a thick Belgian accent, and my muddled brain was trying to piece together his sentences.

"I am going to do another ultrasound, and we are going to try and see what is happening with your baby. I can tell you that from what I have heard so far, this looks to be an extremely serious situation. What are you thinking, sweetheart?"

I said the first thing that came to mind, and I said it with much more conviction than I was feeling.

"I think my Jesus is the same as He was before I walked through that door." I looked him dead in the eye, willing myself to believe it.

I knew it was true, and I needed to hear the words, even if they were coming from my own mouth.

He patted my leg and nodded, moving away from me and toward the machine. When Todd and his mom came back in, I was in too much shock to cry. As my mother-in-law hugged me, I kept saying over and over, "He is still the same, Mom. He hasn't changed. He hasn't changed." It was the only thing I could cling to as truth in the madness of the moment.

It was quickly apparent from the hushed whispers and pointing that the doctor was going to confirm our worst fears. After consulting with his partner for a few minutes (in German, to add to the surreal nature of the moment), he turned to us and after a thought-ful pause said the words no parent ever wants to hear.

"Your daughter has many conditions that are not compatible with life. She does not have functioning kidneys, there is no amni-otic fluid, and her heart is incredibly enlarged. It appears to be taking up more than 80 percent of her chest, so there will be no room for lungs to grow. We also do not believe she has a bladder or a stomach, and I cannot see four chambers in her heart."

He paused and took a deep breath before delivering the final blow.

"You will have some choices to make, which our counselor will discuss with you in a moment, but the bottom line is that this child cannot survive."

My mind is a little fuzzy on the next few minutes because I was making a conscious effort not to pass out. It was too much to process, too much to try and incorporate into reality. I have read about situations like this, and I didn't understand what people meant when they said they felt like they were watching their own lives.

I do now.

I slipped into a part of myself I never knew existed. There were voices, movements, questions, and the man I love—all of it. But they were moving around me, and I couldn't figure out how to be present with them. I really believe that the Lord held me together by shielding me from the reality of the situation. I knew it was bad but through a blurry lens.

I do remember the doctor saying something about how my body would have a different shape when I went home. I didn't process what he was saying right away, and in my confused state I nodded with him, seemingly agreeing with his suggestion to terminate the pregnancy.

They walked out of the room and told us to come to the room next door when we were ready.

I heard my mother-in-law whispering, pleading, *"No, no Jesus. Please, no. Oh, Lord, no."*

I couldn't find the strength to cry.

Todd helped me wipe off the cold jelly while we stared at the blank screen. The room was silent in a way I have never experienced silence. He held up my maternity pants for me as I eased my way back into them, filling the panel with my growing stomach.

We looked at each other as he put my shirt on. He pulled my arms through the holes like I was a rag doll, and we spoke a thousand words that were never heard in this world as we both started to come to terms with what was happening. He put my head on his chest, and as much as I'm sure he wanted to tell me everything was going to be OK, there was really no point.

We both knew it wouldn't.

A few minutes later we were shuffled into a small room where a genetic counselor recommended terminating the pregnancy. She was as kind as she was direct and not a stranger to my situation. She herself had lost four babies, having carried two to term knowing that the baby would die. She said she could not recommend that option to me and that the experience had shattered her.

Dr. J agreed. Given the severity of Audrey's malformations, there was simply no hope for survival, so why put off the inevitable? It would just make it harder on everyone. While they were talking, I looked out the window at the people below and thought it was so strange that life looked normal. Todd's voice faded into the background as I watched everyone hurrying to lunch, hurrying to work, hurrying to their cars. I have such a vivid recollection of that moment as I asked myself why I had spent so much time hurrying, and there I was in the place where time stood still.

I can't tell you how long the conversation lasted. I know much of it consisted of my listening and nodding to give the impression that I understood what she was saying. To a certain extent I did, and I trusted her expertise, but Audrey's movements distracted me; they were a constant reminder of the life that hadn't given up yet.

Both the counselor and the doctor gave us the impression that Audrey would likely be in increasing pain as she grew because she was trapped in the confines of my fluid-less womb. That thought terrified me. They described her hands and feet being twisted and lodged within me, and I wondered if it might be better to just let her go to the Lord now instead of putting her through all of that.

We would do anything to take her pain away. Although we learned later there was no reason to believe she was in pain, at the time we just wanted to do whatever would be easiest on her.

Todd and I told them we would at least like to have a second opinion before we made up our minds. They were happy to allow that. I hugged the geneticist and told her that I was grateful that she had been so kind to me and had opened up about her experiences. I have actually never shared this, but as I am writing, I am remembering that as I reached out to her, I had a brief daydream of bringing Audrey to see her in a few months. As my mind wandered, I thought about how powerful it would be if the Lord healed her and I could introduce the two of them. I felt a fleeting moment of hope as we said good-bye. Even in that desperate place, I felt the Lord urging me not to succumb to my fears.

I was hoping that Dr. F, my high-risk doctor from my pregnancy with the twins, would be available for counsel. However, he is an internationally recognized specialist, and his schedule allows him little time in the local hospital. We went up two floors to my obstetrician's office, and they had received the news before we got there. They were already in tears. After so many years together, they had become like family to us. My obstetrician came in the room, and we asked his opinion. He agreed that the report did not look at all promising. I asked if there was any chance that I could see Dr. F since he was a specialist in these types of situations. He agreed that would be the best plan but thought the chances of it happening were slim. He agreed to make the phone call and see when Dr. F would be on call next.

A few minutes later he came back into the room and told us that by some fluke (we don't call it that, do we?) they had told him that if I checked in that evening, he would be able to see me the next morning. I will never forget the words Dr. T said to me that day before we left.

"This baby has something I cannot fix. Miracles are the Lord's business." He tucked my chart into his white coat and exited quietly, reverently. Somehow this inexplicable peace continued to cover me, reminding me that the same God who raised people from the dead was forming my Audrey in the "secret place" (Ps. 139:15).

I have clear memories of what happened next, because it is really the moment I emotionally connected with what was happening. We got to the car and my fingers numbly dialed Audra. She was waiting to hear how my doctor's appointment went, assuming that I was calling with good news. She answered cheerfully, and I burst into tears—sobbing, shaking, screaming, unintelligibly crying. She listened for a minute, and before she even understood the situation, she was packing her car to come and meet me at my house.

By the time we got home, my entire family was waiting with puffy, reddened, shocked faces. We gathered them together and slowly retold the events of the day. As we spoke, my nearly ninety-year-old grandmother shook her head and moved her fingers along an invisible rosary. My sister-in-law took our children to her house so that we could pack and have some time to process before we explained the situation to them.

I was so distraught that I fell into a deep sleep on the couch while the quiet, sad voices danced around me. When I awoke, it was dark, and I was totally disoriented. Todd was sitting at my feet. It took me a minute to remember what was going on.

"We need to pack our things and get going, baby," he whispered.

It was really happening.

About an hour later we checked ourselves into the hospital while the receptionists tried to keep their emotions under control. After all, what do you say to a mother whose baby is dying in her womb?

They checked us into our room, and Todd opened the curtains to let the city lights in. Neither of us said a word as we realized the view from our room was eye to eye with the hotel where we had celebrated our wedding reception just six years prior. We collapsed into each other's arms and wailed, thinking of all we didn't know on the night we had said those precious words: *For better or for worse . . . in sickness and in health . . .*

We both wondered if maybe what they had seen was just a mistake, maybe a bad angle or something. We had each had a sense of hope that the diagnosis was wrong, that Audrey was a healthy, thriving baby after all. Being back in the hospital was awful, and we both hated every moment of it. All of the horrible memories of being there with Abby and Ellie came floating back to me. The sound the bed made when it moved, the smell of the hospital soap, the tiny neonatal bed that sat in an adjacent room, reminding us that we would probably not have the chance to put her in it—it was all unbearable. Todd climbed in the tiny twin bed with me, and we lay with our arms wrapped around each other, waiting for the morning to bring hope to us.

When daybreak finally came, Dr. F walked into my hospital room and smiled gently when he saw me.

"Angie, I was kind of hoping I wouldn't see you again."

"Me, too, Dr. F, but I'm really glad it's you."

We both forced smiles.

Since he only sees women in such dire situations, it was a mixed blessing to be in each other's presence. It didn't take him and his assistant long to confirm the previous findings through ultrasound and reiterate that Audrey could not survive. He was kind and tender with his words and his actions, but the truth is the truth no matter how you dress it up.

She isn't going to be yours.

His suggestion was to carry the baby, not because he thought she would live but rather because he knew where we stood in our faith. We nodded in response, both of us knowing that this was really the only option we would consider. We had talked about it after the appointment the day before, and we knew there was no way we were going to take her life. He explained that there was a good chance she would die in the womb. We told him we would cross that bridge if we came to it.

She was our daughter and we would fight for her.

We told him that we believed him and that we trusted him. We also explained in no uncertain terms that our faith was in a Physician Who hadn't fully expressed His will for Audrey, and we would wait for that diagnosis.

I got a message a few days later from the student who had been doing rounds with Dr. F and was in the room for our exam. He told me that our conversation reminded him of how great his God was and that as he left our room he decided to commit to practicing fetal medicine. I saved the e-mail he wrote, amazed at the impact those few moments had made on him. He went on to say that Audrey would forever be a part of his career and would remind him every day that every life is a life worth fighting for.

He closed his note by thanking Audrey for changing his life.

I got chills as I finished reading.

At the time we had no idea how often we would hear that sentence from strangers.

In the days after Audrey was diagnosed, I began to see Scripture with new eyes. I was desperate for truth in the midst of the chaos. I began to search for stories of healing in hopes of peace. One day in my quiet time, I read the story of Lazarus, and it felt like a sweet balm to my bitter hurt (John 11).

I can only imagine what it must have been like to sit at Jesus' feet and worship Him. I often wonder if I would have truly believed He was who He said He was. Martha and her sister Mary did believe in Him, and we know from Scripture that Jesus had a fondness for their family, including their brother Lazarus. In the book of John, we read that Lazarus had become ill, and in their desperation Mary and Martha sent word to Jesus that he was sick. The letter they sent contained only a few telling words, "Lord, the one you love is sick" (John 11:3).

I became fascinated by their message to the Lord as I struggled with how to pray for my daughter. The Greek word translated *Lord* in this passage is *kyrios* and denotes sovereignty. In other words, Martha and Mary are calling out to Jesus as the One who has the power to heal, recognizing His dominion over everything, including life and death. The word *kyrios* was commonly used to indicate etiquette when speaking to someone to whom you are subservient. Martha and Mary knew who He was, and they wanted Him to know that they did. A plea offered in submission and humility to the One who holds the fate of their brother in His hands—what a beautiful image of trust.

What Mary and Martha say in their message to Jesus is not as interesting to me as what they *don't* say. They don't refer to Lazarus by name, nor do they ask Him to heal their brother. While we can infer that they were conveying a need for help, they don't actually ask Him to do anything specific. This request is similar to the one that Mary, the mother of Jesus, made at the wedding feast in Cana. We are told that as the wine started to run out, she said to Jesus, "They have no more wine." She doesn't explicitly tell Him the solution she is looking for but rather states the problem and waits to see what He will do about it.

As I read their words, it occurred to me that this is not the way I approach the Lord with a crisis. I run to Him with a laundry list of suitable responses and beg Him to accommodate me.

"Heal her heart, Lord."

"Make her kidneys work."

"Let her live."

I am pretty comfortable saying He is in complete control until the ground grows weak beneath me. At that point I tell Him what He should do to fix it. While I know there isn't anything wrong with asking God to intervene, there is a gentle surrender that I was drawn to in this story.

Recognize who He is—*kyrios*—and tell Him the problem.

Leave the rest to Him.

As we will discover later, there is always room for doubt wherever God has made a way for faith. Yet in this moment Mary and Martha simply called out to Him.

And so did we.

A few days before my ultrasound, I had seen a stuffed bunny in a little shop and asked Todd if we could buy it for Audrey. It was a little pricey, so he told me maybe we could come back for it. For some reason I kept thinking about it, and after we left the hospital with her confirmed diagnosis, I told Todd I wanted to go back and get it. He said he had actually been thinking the same thing.

We walked into the shop and headed back to the toy section, both of us silently noting that the bunny wasn't on the shelf where it had been. We searched for a moment, and then I heard Todd say something behind me. I turned around and saw him grabbing little bunny ears from a barrel of toys. As he lifted it out, we both gasped. It had a permanent black mark over its heart. I started crying and pulled the bunny to my chest as people shuffled past us, lost in their normal lives. When we got to the counter, the saleswoman started to scratch off the mark.

"It isn't going to come off," Todd said, choking back tears.

"No, I don't think it is. We have others back there. Want me to grab one?" She looked at me and then at him.

Neither of us tried to explain.

"No, we'll take this one, thank you." Todd managed a half-hearted smile and shook his head from side to side when she offered a discount.

"No thank you, ma'am. We want to pay the regular price." Todd smiled at her, and she began wrapping the pink tissue paper around our bunny, gently slipping it into the gift bag.

I am sure she was wondering why we wanted to pay full price for a damaged toy, but it made perfect sense to us.

After all, she was *our* bunny.

We went to a local pizza restaurant and discussed what we were going to do about telling the kids. We cried through the whole meal, and our sweet waitress didn't know what to say. I realized that I was entering a new phase of life, one where my body belied the truth, leaving the dilemma of how to share that with the world.

After a few hours of talking, we got some of our thoughts together. Before we left, I looked at Todd and said, "He may give us today with her, or He may give us the rest of our lives. Either way, we are going to be purposeful, and we are going to live it to the fullest. She is our child, and we are going to love her with the same intensity we love our other girls. It is all we have."

Todd agreed, and we took our to-go boxes (not surprisingly, neither of us were actually very hungry) and headed home to talk to our girls.

When we got there, we told the kids that we needed to talk to them about something. We all sat down and I put the Audrey Bunny on a little white chair in the center of the family room.

The girls gathered around us and waited patiently. They had been at their cousins' house and had an idea that something was wrong but didn't know what it was. They looked at us with fear in their eyes, and as long as I live, I will never forget the feeling I had, knowing I was about to tell them that their sister was going to die. I took a deep breath and asked the Lord to fill my mouth with wisdom. Todd sat beside me, and I began to tell them the story.

"Girls, Mommy and Daddy went to the doctor today, and they told us some sad news about baby Audrey." They looked curious. They were only two and five at the time. What could be wrong with a little baby? They listened with expressions of confusion as I continued.

"See how this bunny has a boo-boo on her heart?" They nodded.

"So does our Audrey Girl. And they don't think that she will be able to come and sleep in her crib here because she is very sick and she will probably go right to Jesus after she's born."

I was trying to gauge how they were receiving what I had said so far, so I asked if they had any questions.

Ellie raised her hand.

"Yes, honey."

"Is it *for sure*, Mommy?"

I thought for a minute about how I wanted to answer her. What a delicate balance between what medicine tells us and what we know our God is capable of doing. I didn't want to give them false hope, but I also wanted them to feel safe believing in the healing power of our Lord.

"Well, Ellie, some very smart people have told us that it *is* for sure. But God is bigger than them, and if He decides to fix her, then He can do that."

She nodded, and I could tell that she had already begun her prayers for healing.

She needed permission to hope.

We all did actually.

"But since Audrey has this boo-boo right now, I want us to put some bandages on her heart to remember to pray for her. We don't know if God is going to make her better or not, but *we will keep believing that He can.*"

And so began the story of Audrey Bunny.

As the girls put Band-Aids over her heart, we prayed silently, and each in our own way, we spoke to the God of miracles, the One who still hears us all these years later.

Lord, the one You love is sick . . .

I am worn out from [all my] groaning;
all night long I flood my bed with weeping
and drench my couch with tears.
My eyes grow weak with sorrow.
Psalm 6:6–7

Ah, Sovereign LORD, you have made the
heavens and the earth by your great
power and outstretched arm. Nothing is
too hard for you. . . . O great and
powerful God, whose name is
the LORD Almighty, great are your purposes
and mighty are your deeds.
Jeremiah 32:17–19

Chapter 3
The One Who Can

"Hope" is the thing with feathers
That perches in the soul—
And sings the tune without words
And never stops—at all.
—Emily Dickinson

The days after Audrey's diagnosis were some of the hardest. I would wake up in the morning, and it would hit me over and over again that it was real. It seemed that every encounter with other people was so weighed down by the reality of my hurt that I could barely stand it. I avoided the never-ending phone calls, asking Todd to take over because I simply couldn't talk about it anymore.

I decided to start writing a blog to keep our friends and family updated and to avoid the agony of having to retell everything over and over. It was good therapy for me to sit on my bed in silence and pour my heart out to the keyboard. I didn't have to see the look in people's eyes or watch them uncomfortably search for the right words when we both knew there just weren't any.

Within a few days of the doctor's appointment, we spoke to our pastor, and he arranged a prayer meeting at our church. I will never forget sitting in a circle with many of the deacons and several friends as they offered prayers to the Lord on our behalf. I remember that evening being one of peace, and as each person spoke, the conviction in my spirit grew stronger. I felt more at ease than I imagined I could in such a situation. They read pertinent Scriptures in hushed tones as if the Lord Himself were sitting among us.

And He was.

As the intensity of our meeting rose, a storm raged outside. At one point, as someone was praying, the door blew open, and rain started pouring into the room. Two men struggled to close the doors as the wind relentlessly forced them open.

I felt like the Holy Spirit was speaking to all of us as the men finally sat, wiping their soaked faces. The Lord was in the rain. He was in the prayer.

He was in it all.

He wanted His presence known as this body of believers gathered on behalf of a little girl who would most likely never even get to see the church with her own eyes. That night I realized that, while I am an independent person who struggles with asking for help, this was a situation where I wasn't going to have that liberty. I sat, fully humbled, as many I love spoke wisdom over me, and I admitted to myself that I was going to need help to get through this season of life.

Later that same week my dear friend Julie had a baby shower for the little girl she was expecting, and I couldn't stand to miss it. Everyone there knew what was going on with me, and we all danced around it so that it wouldn't dampen the spirit of the party. Julie isn't the kind of person who operates well in the world of pretending. She is incredibly authentic and never shies away from whatever conversation will lead into the deep places.

I know that night was as torturous as it was beautiful for her, as she opened tiny pink onesies and bibs. Surrounded by gifts, her eyes searched mine as we all did our best to get through the night. At one point we gathered around her and took turns praying over her sweet baby. As petitions for a healthy child and a smooth delivery filled the room, I felt my heart start to pound. Audrey was kicking me gently, persistently, and the tears started to fall. Audra and my friend Jessica held my hands, and before we knew it, a sniffling noise filled the room. It was hard to tell if they were tears of joy or of sorrow.

I can distinctly remember the way grief and joy danced together as if they had a right to.

As the prayer time ended, I knew I needed to leave. My face was beet red, and as much as I knew nobody begrudged me for it, I didn't want to take away from the celebration. Everyone started to move into the kitchen for snacks, and I walked over to Julie to say good-night. Her makeup was smudged, and her eyes were wet with agony. She grabbed me and pulled me to her. As our stomachs pressed against each other, we both broke down and sobbed.

She kept whispering how sorry she was, and I just buried my head in her shoulder and let it out, grasping for sanity in the chaos. After a few minutes I snuck out the front door and fumbled with my car keys for what seemed like forever. As I drove away, I saw Julie through the windows wiping her face, the whole house lit up like Christmas while I sat in my quiet car.

As I drove, I began to pound the steering wheel and scream. I literally beat it with my fists and wailed as I begged the Lord to heal her.

"You can do it, God. If You wanted to, You could fix her. **FIX HER. FIX HER.** . . . *Oh, Lord, fix her.*"

It was storming out, and as the windshield wipers cleared just enough rain for me to see the road, I let myself shout until I was weak. I continued to shake for the rest of the drive, and it was one of the first times I remember really allowing myself to feel the unbelievable agony of what I was facing. It was also one of the first times I would say I sensed Him there, right beside me.

All-knowing.

Perfect.

Redeemer.

The One who *can*.

I embraced something that night that I will never forget, and it has continued to shape my walk with Him. He isn't threatened by my heartbreak and questioning any more than He is threatened by a rainstorm.

He knows that rain will fall.

He knows that I will fall.

And so, on a long drive home, I gave my deepest hurt to the Father who wanted nothing less than every bit of it.

What I needed to learn about myself was clear in that moment. *I did believe in Him enough to call out.* I trusted Him enough to share the brokenness, even though He already knew it all. I thought about what it must feel like not only to know that one of your children is hurting but what it would mean to you if she told you herself—if she came to you because she wanted it to be a shared grief.

And so as the rain fell, the wipers wiped, and the Lord listened, I let Him into a place I had never fully invited Him before.

A place of communion where I could rest knowing He heard me.

A place I would reside for months to come.

We made a point of including Audrey in the most mundane parts of life. I told her about the way the washer spun our clothes around and took long, warm showers talking to her about her daddy and sisters. I rocked her, sang to her, and rubbed my belly when I felt her scooting around. She was usually the most active when I was lying in bed, and when I knew she was awake, I read Scripture to her and told her about the great King Jesus and the way He loved her.

I told her that she could trust Him and that He would take better care of her than we could.

I said it, but I didn't always feel it.

It is hard to accept that anyone, even the God of the universe, could love your child the way that you do.

I spent hours staring at her profile on my ultrasound pictures, and all I could see were her perfect nose and lips. I tried to stop myself from getting too caught up in daydreams about her swinging in the backyard or tasting ice cream for the first time. There was no room to consider the cost of investing my heart; I was already head over heels in love with her.

She was Audrey.

Fourth daughter of Todd and Angie Smith.

Sister to Ellie, Abby, and Sarah Kate.

She was ours.

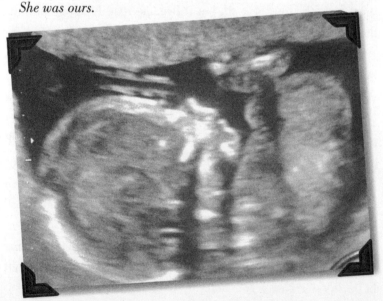

We reveled in the things I hadn't even noticed in my other pregnancies, like the fact that she tended to kick more after I ate a peanut butter and jelly sandwich. It was such a tender time. We didn't want to miss a moment of it, and as a family we loved her the only way we knew how.

I bought the girls disposable cameras so they could document the way they were experiencing the whole thing. When we developed the film, we found dozens of pictures of my stomach in the most random places: the grocery store, a children's play, the park, the beach, and so on. When I asked them about it, they explained that they were pictures of Audrey for a photo album so she could remember all of the places we had taken her.

Sometimes we just sat around the kitchen table and painted silently while they processed a tough morning. Afterwards we would talk about what they were feeling and how we could be praying. Other times we would make some hot chocolate and snuggle for a quiet time while they "read" their Bible stories and Todd and I poured over Scripture.

We had so many conversations about how we could protect them from the hurt of it all, but it became readily apparent to us that the Lord was taking good care of their hearts. They saw me crying on many occasions, despite the fact that I didn't want to burden them, and they responded with wisdom well beyond their years. We wanted them to feel safe in their sadness and spent a good deal of time just listening. They asked us hard questions that no parent wants to answer, but I believe the Lord graced us with a presence that defied the information. At the end of every day, regardless of what it had held, we knew that she had been given to us for a purpose, and we were seeking wisdom as we embraced that.

To be brutally honest, it wasn't because embracing it came naturally. It was because we didn't know how to survive without believing that God was in control.

So many people have asked us how we got through those first weeks after Audrey's diagnosis. I want to say that we were always strong in the Lord and that we relied fully on Him, but the truth is we were stunned with pain. Some days just thinking about getting out of bed or going to the grocery was hard because we could hardly walk anywhere without being a spectacle.

My twins look younger than they are, and when people would see three small girls and a swollen belly, they could hardly resist making comments. An overwhelming amount of the time they were sweet, but I still felt a sting when they said, "Another one so soon?" or, "Finally a boy this time?"

Most of the time I retreated emotionally and nodded without further explanation, but I can recall an incident while I was out one day that sent me for a loop emotionally. I looked up, and all of a sudden a woman was standing in front of us, alternately staring at my kids and my stomach with a look of disdain.

"I'm guessing this one was an 'oops'?"

I wasn't prepared for what rose up in me, but I stared at her, eye to eye, and more pointedly than I had intended. I replied, "There is nothing about this child that is an 'oops.' *Nothing*."

I don't think she knew what to make of my response, so I shuffled the girls ahead of me and held her gaze long enough to pray that God would convict me before I opened my mouth again. I think the good Lord knew that if I had been banned from Target, things would go downhill fast.

So she kept walking.

On other occasions someone with kind eyes would ask when I was due, or whether or not I knew what I was having, and it felt wrong not to tell them the whole story. It was really hard to talk about it over and over, so I developed a script that I used when I felt like I might have an opportunity to share my faith with others. Basically I said that we were expecting our fourth daughter and that her name was Audrey Caroline but she was not expected to survive. Inevitably people's faces would be painted with a combination of sadness and confusion. Usually, if I waited a moment, they would ask why I was continuing the pregnancy.

I have to admit, the first few times this happened, I was a little surprised by their frankness. Yet it actually became a welcomed question when I realized that it was an opportunity to share the gospel. Truth be told, anyone who has ever met me will tell you that I don't know how to chitchat. I'm the lady waiting behind you in the grocery line who asks how old your kids are and within about ten minutes I am asking about your deepest life wounds. While I have never been shy about sharing my faith, I am not one to push it in a way that feels uninvited either. The beauty of this situation was that people were so moved by the fact that I had chosen this route that they wanted to understand why.

What better way to talk about the Lord?

I'm sure several people considered me a nutcase to have such delusional faith in the same God who appeared to be allowing my daughter to die in the first place, but that wasn't the typical response. Sharing my story opened so many doors to conversation that would never have taken place.

She was already ministering, and she hadn't left the womb.

My sweet, sweet Audrey.

The churning inside me never stops;
days of suffering confront me.
Job 30:27

But now, this is what the LORD says—he
who created you, O Jacob, he who formed you,
O Israel: "Fear not, for I have redeemed you;
I have summoned you by name; you are mine.
When you pass through the waters,
I will be with you; and when you
pass through the rivers,
they will not sweep over you.
When you walk through the fire,
you will not be burned;
the flames will not set you ablaze.
For I am the LORD, your God,
the Holy One of Israel, your Savior."
Isaiah 43:1–3

Chapter 4
Three Days

When you are sorrowful look again in your heart, and you shall see that in truth you are weeping for that which has been your delight.

Some of you say, "Joy is greater than sorrow," and others say, "Nay, sorrow is the greater."

But I say unto you, they are inseparable.

Together they come, and when one sits alone with you at your board, remember that the other is asleep upon your bed.

Verily you are suspended like scales between your sorrow and your joy.
—Kahlil Gibran

We know from commentaries on the story of Lazarus that after He received Mary and Martha's letter, the Lord waited another two full days before beginning His journey to Judea. Many scholars have speculated wise and meaningful reasons for this delay, one of the most common being the belief that a person's soul hovered around his or her body for three days after death, so in essence a person wasn't really considered dead until after that period. As I read Scripture, I could imagine why the Lord chose to do what He did; Jesus wanted them to know that what He was about to do was not a clever magic trick but a miracle of epic proportion.

As I tried to imagine what it must have felt like to be Mary and Martha, I so easily associated with their limited viewpoint. They have sent word they trust will be received by the Lord who loves them. They know that He will recognize the urgency in their voices and surely will come and heal their beloved brother. Each morning they wake to another seemingly hopeless day, watching the hours tick by until eventually they begin to lose hope. They weren't given an explanation. They didn't know the outcome or the reasoning. They sat in silence and hurt because they felt like the only One who could make it right had abandoned them.

I am sure that somewhere along the way they wondered if they had angered or offended Jesus.

Maybe He was punishing them for something they had done in the past.

Maybe He was too busy.

Maybe He didn't care.

Maybe they just didn't matter to Him as much as they thought they did.

Maybe He wasn't powerful enough for this situation.

Maybe He wasn't who He said He was after all.

However theologically flawed they were, all of those thoughts entered my mind during my pregnancy. On dark nights when the rest of the neighborhood was asleep, I was awake, battling with my brokenness and asking Him why He wouldn't come. I have no doubt that Satan was thriving on my angst and doing everything he could to convince me that I had been forsaken.

Have you been there?

In the dark of night, it is easy to surrender to the lies.

What Mary and Martha could not see is what the Lord was doing and how He was responding to the situation. In John 11:14–15, Jesus tells His disciples that Lazarus is dead but that He is glad He wasn't there so that they will be able to witness the miracle and believe.

Think about this for a minute.

The letter that Jesus has received from the sisters says that Lazarus is *sick*, not that he has died.

The Lord knew exactly what was happening to Lazarus just like he knew exactly what was happening to Audrey. Yet we, just like Mary and Martha, are not privy to His thoughts.

Sometimes He just feels so faraway and so indifferent from where we are. Of course we see glimpses of Him and reasons to believe. Yet we are human. We want to *know* He is coming. I found so much solace in relating to what they must have felt because I was feeling it as well.

In the midst of the waiting, we went to frequent doctors appointments and ultrasounds, and we wondered what He was doing behind the scenes. They wanted to keep a close eye on me, despite the fact that there was no chance of substantial change in her diagnosis, so three weeks after Audrey's diagnosis, we went back in for an ultrasound. The night before we went, Todd and I lay in bed praying, and we asked the Lord to be present at our appointment. We whispered our hopes into the night, no matter how ridiculous they seemed. After we prayed, I rolled over in bed while my hands cupped my stomach, and I begged Him to give us some sign that He knew our hearts and that He was listening.

I wanted to feel like He was going to respond to our cries.

"Please, Lord. I need to know You are coming; I am waiting, but I am exhausted with grief."

Once more, I closed my eyes and prayed I would see His face in the morning.

As she began the scan, the sweet, seasoned technician appeared a little caught off guard.

"Well, wow. Look at that."

We looked, but it was just a mass of black-and-white movement to us.

"Here is her bladder, hon." She squeezed some more goop on me and continued looking.

Todd leaned in toward the screen, eyes squinted.

"They told us that she didn't have . . ." He never finished because he was too distracted by the possibilities that were floating in his head.

So was I.

A few more minutes passed as we watched Audrey hiccupping and moving her arms. The technician paused again and began to zoom in on something else.

"Here's her . . . well, here's her stomach." She didn't make eye contact and she looked completely perplexed.

Todd and I glanced at each other in confusion.

"We were told she didn't have a stomach," Todd said quietly.

"Yes, that's what they told me as well, but here it is." She pointed at the screen, and we looked at our baby in awe.

Could it be that nothing was what it seemed? At the very least, things were different from what we initially thought, and we braced ourselves in prayer as the exam continued. My heart was beating out of my chest as I waited.

"Lord, the one You love is sick . . ."

The technician's eyes were transfixed on the monitor as she drifted to Audrey's kidneys, which were one of the two issues that made her "incompatible with life." We were prepared to hear that she had more cysts than she had before because that was common with babies who had been diagnosed with polycystic kidneys. Not only were there not more cysts, but it also appeared that one of them was cyst-free. Medically we had been told this was impossible. At the very least it was counter to her diagnosis, and at this point my hands started sweating. I gripped the sides of the bed as she moved the wand over Audrey's heart, another issue that was life-threatening.

I could see the beating, but I couldn't make out details. I knew what she was looking for, so I depended on her face for cues. She moved her wand until she got the exact angle she wanted, and a look of restrained shock came across her face. She swallowed deliberately and cleared her throat, obviously unsure of how to tell us what she was seeing.

"Todd, Angie. I don't know what to tell you except for what I am seeing here, and I can't really explain any of it."

She paused and looked me in the eye before she spoke.

"She has four chambers in her heart."

I felt like the air left the room as Todd and I stared at each other, wide-eyed with the most unpredicted glimpse of hope we had ever experienced. I burst into tears.

Todd squeezed my hand and asked the technician what all of this meant. She explained that she really wasn't prepared to answer that question. She wanted the doctors to look over the scans in the morning and call me when they had had a chance to try and make sense of them. I sobbed the whole way to the car and through every phone call I made for the next hour. They were the grateful tears of a mother who had never been appropriately awed by the fact that a heart could have four chambers or that a baby had a stomach. They were the tears of a mother who was just beginning to understand how much she had taken for granted in this life.

We celebrated my nephew's eleventh birthday that night, and we laughed and cried over burgers and miracles. All the kids took home balloons from the restaurant, and Kate became particularly connected to hers.

When I say "connected," what I mean is, "screaming bloody murder when anyone touched, approached, or looked at her balloon." After all the candles were blown out and the house was quiet, Todd called me into Kate's room, where she was (finally) sleeping. She was clearly in dreamland, but in her left hand she was gripping the balloon string as the object of her affection floated unassumably over her head.

That is so Kate, I thought.

After I laughed for a minute, it occurred to me that she was doing exactly what we are.

Against all odds she was refusing to let go.

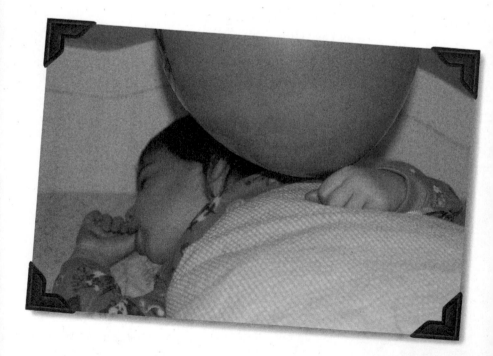

Like Mary and Martha, I was reluctant to give up hope. When I read Scripture, I try to see it in my mind. I tried to put myself into each story as an observer, trying to taste what they did, smell what they did, see the world the way they did. I imagine the sisters spoke often during that time, questioning each other, wondering how the other was processing the situation. They probably checked the city gates several times a day and looked for any signs of Him they could find, possibly asking those around them if they had seen anything that might lead them to believe He was coming.

We took many opportunities during this time to read Bible stories to the girls, illustrating the ways God had come through for His people in miraculous ways. We also talked extensively about the times that He didn't. I really believe the Lord spoke to them in ways we will never fully understand because sometimes their insights were so far beyond their ages that the only possible explanation was that the Holy Spirit had granted them wisdom.

One night we were reading the story of Abraham and Isaac in our favorite children's Bible, and all three of them were riveted. We got to the part where Abraham raises his knife while Isaac lies motionless, tied up in rope that his father's hands have wrapped around him. The girls always hold their breath just before God says, "Stop!" They know the outcome because we have read it to them many times, but their expressions always stay the same until the moment when he is loosened and set free.

The next day I was in the kitchen with Ellie, and she was stirring cake batter while I cleaned. I asked her to tell me the story from the night before, and she did a remarkably good job recalling what happened. Just before she got to God's dramatic rescue, she paused and looked at me like she had something to say.

"Mommy?"

"What, honey?"

"You know that part where God yells stop?"

I nodded, half paying attention.

"I don't think He is going to say that to you."

My hands stopped moving, and I looked in her eyes.

Sad, knowing, feeling, see-into-your-soul eyes.

"I don't know that He is, Ellie."

For what seemed like forever, we just continued our motions in silence. I don't know that I can adequately describe what that moment was to me. It was just one of those times in life when you know that God is speaking.

I couldn't stop thinking about it.

It was His son.

His hands.

His rope.

And yet it was never His at all.

When people talked to me about what I was going through, they often used the word *trial*. I think it was the right word. In the thousands of years since Abraham and Isaac, the rules have not changed. We listen, we praise, we walk in the direction of God's voice, and we obey.

It's that simple.

Sometimes that means we get to unbind and celebrate.

Sometimes it means we don't.

That night I looked up the original Hebrew word for *trial* in one of my big fancy books (OK, one of *Todd's* fancy books). I hope that as you read these words, you will know the way He quieted me in that moment.

> TRIAL (Old Testament) *noun: from the Hebrew word* sara *which comes from the root* srh, *which means, "to bind, tie up, restrict." Thus, the noun*

*comes to denote **a narrow place in life where one is bound or restricted . . .***

I carried this image with me for days, saturating myself in the truth that I discovered about what it means to be walking where I was. I thought of sweet Audrey, unable to grow, restricted, as bound and helpless as Isaac. As we walked this "narrow place," I was reminded of the power of being still and submitting to the God I trusted more than I ever thought I could. During these days I walked moment by moment with the God of the universe.

The God who chose Abraham.

The God who chose me.

I couldn't think of anyone I would feel safer with because, of course, the difficult, terrible, beautiful truth is that He Himself is not unfamiliar with the binding.

I bore my wounds tenderly, with worship ever on my lips because He did the same for me.

> *But he was pierced for our transgressions, he was crushed for our iniquities; the punishment that brought us peace was upon him, and by his wounds we are healed. (Isa. 53:5)*

It is so hard to be in those three days.

Constantly vigilant for His reappearance, jumping at any chance we get to see His face, vacillating between what the world is telling us is real and what we know is true about our Jesus. And all the while He is just waiting for the time that is right.

He hasn't forgotten, nor has He abandoned us.

We can rest knowing that not only has He heard us but that when the time is right, He will walk the long road to Judea and bring glory to His father.

He will redeem what seemed hopeless.

And so, with the taste of praise already on our tongues, we waited for the One who loved her.

Little did we know He had already begun His journey.

As you do not know the path of the wind,
or how the body is formed in a mother's womb,
so you cannot understand the work of God,
the Maker of all things.
Ecclesiastes 11:5

Remember your word to your servant,
for you have given me hope.
My comfort in my suffering is this:
Your promise preserves my life.
Psalm 119:49–50

Chapter 5

The Castle

If I find in myself a desire which no
experience in this world can satisfy,
the most probable explanation is that
I was made for another world.
—C. S. Lewis

Late one evening we were talking to the girls about the fact
that while Audrey was in my tummy, we needed to do all
the things with her that we would want to do with a baby sister
who was already here. We asked them what kinds of things they
wanted to teach her, and they thought for a while. Eventually Ellie
piped up and said, "I want her to see Cinderella's castle."

We had never been to Disney World before, and despite the
fact that we had neither the budget nor any idea of how to do that
on such short-term notice, we decided to give it a shot. A friend
of ours asked his sister who was a travel agent to help us, and
against all odds, we worked out a trip for later that same month.
When we told our families about what we were going to do, they
decided that if it was OK with us, they would like to join us on

this special trip. A huge group of us made our way into the Magic Kingdom just a few weeks later. We spent our time there laughing and celebrating as a family. We rode everything we could stuff into a day, and then we watched fireworks dance in the sky. I remember talking to a woman who sat next to me during the fireworks because she asked me when I was due and whether I knew what I was having or not. I gave her a brief synopsis of the story, and she covered her mouth in shock and then told me about her own miscarriages.

Even from the beginning, I was amazed at how many women I met had been through miscarriage or infant loss, and what a powerful, connecting experience it is to be able to share with another woman who has been there. So as we sat in the "happiest place on Earth," two strangers mourned the other's losses. As fireworks exploded, we cried. We saw each other for what we were—women who were often just going through the motions of normalcy, partly for our children and partly for ourselves. I began to realize that this was going to be a part of my new life because the world has a way of going on all around you even when you are in the depths of sorrow that belie its pace and fervor.

Shortly after we returned, I blogged about how symbolic this trip had been for me:

February 1, 2008

While we were at Disney World, I was struck by the fact that for a lot of the trip, I just felt sad. I have debated about whether or not to even share this story because we really had a great time, with more memories made than I could ever fit into this blog. My children laughed and rode and ate and stared. They marveled at the castle the way I did when I was a little girl. To our surprise they rode a roller coaster (hands up) nine times in a row. They could not get enough of "It's a Small World" but quickly decided that the real-life princesses were a combination of creepy and "not really the real princesses." They danced in every wide-open space they came across and devoured enough sugar to keep a small country running. In short, they were as happy as I have ever seen them. I am forever grateful for the moments we got with our girls, but there is a deeper story, and I want you to be a part of it.

On the first full day we were there, the girls rode the teacups. My father-in-law and I decided to watch instead of riding. I had the best time seeing everyone loop around the line as they waited for their turn. I was immediately struck by the pattern that emerged. Just as I sat down, I saw a couple arguing over whether or not to ride. They decided to go for it but not before she had leveled him verbally and their little boy was staring off into space. Shortly after, I saw a delicate little flower of a girl stomp on the ground because she wanted the lavender teacup, "NOT the pink!!! AAAHHHH!!!!!" Her mother patted her hair (gently, around the seven-foot bow), and promised they would ride again and again until they secured the coveted cup.

Princess climbed in as another couple started up in the background. They had special tags to ride at a certain time and were irritated that they were going to have to wait another turn. Junior was no more pleased than momma and was the type of child

I try to steer my children away from at the park. He had a look of fierce anger than belied his little body . . . like a live wire in a preschooler, fueled by the attention that he could summon instantaneously. His parents were obviously more worried about his response to the wait than the wait itself.

My suspicions about this particular child were confirmed later in the day when I saw him do the unspeakable while his mother had her back turned.

Are you ready for this?

He spanked Peter Pan's bottom during the Magical Parade.

Oh yes he did.

Don't worry, I gave him a look that could melt ice, and had the victim not been dressed as a magical flying boy-man, I feel confident he would have jumped the rope too.

Anyway, as I watched all of these mini-dramas (and others) unfold, the most beautiful, unusual thing continued to happen.

As soon as the ride started, and the music filled the pavilion, people just forgot why they were unhappy. There was a forty-five-second time period every few minutes where they got lost in the blur of joy. Hands up, screaming laughter, cameras flashing. Even the spanker kid got in on the action.

I love the teacups.

For the better part of the minute, the entire world is just right. It doesn't matter that you waited half an hour or that you pretty much paid $50 for one go-round. It is totally insignificant that your problems are on the other side of the music. Everything is just a whirly-twirly, perfect place.

And then it happens.

Every time.

Go for yourself and watch because, if you let yourself, you will see and feel the moment where the cups slow down and the music surrenders. A collective sigh summarizes the disappointment. Nobody wants it to end; they just want to keep spinning and spinning except that they can't.

It has to end.

You have to get back to life, to hurt, to silence.

To whatever made you run there in the first place.

In a sense that was my experience of the whole park. I wanted to get away, to escape and go somewhere magical, to get caught up in the idea that everything was just right.

I realized about five minutes into the fireworks that I had gotten on a plane to travel to a place where Audrey was healthy.

I cried that night after the lights went out in our room. I talked to the Lord, begged Him to do something, to intervene, to make it right. As He always does, He just sat with me and listened. I felt better (could have been a combination of a Sovereign God and a really high thread count) and eventually fell asleep. When I woke up, I had a message from my amazing nurse practitioner. She is Dr. T's daughter, and I count her as a friend with whom I have traveled for almost six years. She had just gotten the ultrasound report that led us to believe that her original diagnosis might have been wrong.

With bated breath I listened while she explained that although the report noted many encouraging things, the overall picture had not changed.

Medically, Audrey could not survive.

My nurse practitioner is an amazing woman of God, and I know she prays for me. She has traveled around the world to help people in need, and I am sure she has seen her fair share of miracles, so I don't want to give the impression that she intended to leave me without hope. She chose her words carefully, and even in that moment I found myself grateful to a God who always knew that I would stand outside my hotel and cry with a woman who loves Him as much as I do.

Before you toss your Disney brochure or think of me as a fantasy-hating cynic, let me explain.

The happiest place on Earth is not on this Earth.

This life was never meant to fill us or to satisfy our need for goodness.

It wasn't designed to give us an answer but rather to let the question penetrate our lives daily.

I believe that in one way or another God will answer our prayer to heal Audrey. It may not be here, the way we wish it could be, but I have complete faith that she will be whole. And it won't be temporary. If you only hear me say this one thing, all of these words will be worth it. For all of you who want to know the great secret to how we are breathing through this, it is pretty simple.

He is enough.

I am not a preacher. I will not pretend to be. I am a woman who realizes more and more every day that I want Jesus more than I want the teacups to keep spinning. In this life, we are going to be disappointed. We will hurt. But there is great joy in the shadows if you know where to look.

The truth about Disney World, and the entire Disney Empire for that matter, is that it was borne of hurt. Walt Disney was a man with a broken childhood who tried to create a place that mimicked the things he loved as a boy and created the things he always wished he could have had. He worked his entire life to create a world that defied his pain.

If you are hurting right now, I pray that you allow the Great Physician to heal your brokenness as He is healing ours. And if you happen to be enjoying the ride, hold on tight and try not to throw up your lollipop.)

I am celebrating unspeakable joy tonight.

A joy that defies this world and welcomes the next with the eagerness of a child.

Thank You, Lord.

We are humbled by Your deep, unfailing, unending love.

It's hard for me to be where I am today and read over those words. I wanted so badly to be able to escape from all of the sadness, and I learned a lesson about this world that I will never forget.

We won't have it here, friends.

I am sure you have had your fair share of hurt as well, and I wonder, where do you run? It may not be Disney World, but it might be to a bad habit, or to something that fills you up temporarily. It is hard to discover that the cheap imitation of satisfaction we have grown accustomed to is woefully unrepresentative of what awaits us. It is not easy to think of it that way, even for me.

In some ways I wish I could go back to the place where the cotton candy and parades distracted me. In other ways I am relieved to be on this side of life, where I have come to terms (as much as I can) with the fact that in this life, on this Earth, I am going to hunger.

The hunger will not be satisfied. It cannot be. And when the wind blows through my soul and tempts me to despair over the lot I have been given, I cling to the truth that the Lord has something better for me. It won't always be like this. You will know Him fully one day, and all the hurts that consume you in this moment will vanish and be forgotten. I know it sounds crazy. I guess it's crazy to think that a God could love us so much that He would want to create a place to be with Him eternally, where we can revel in His perfection and rest in true peace.

Yet if I speak, my pain is not relieved;
and if I refrain, it does not go away.
Surely, O God, you have worn me out.
Job 16:6–7

Sustain me according to your promise, and I will live;
do not let my hopes be dashed.
Uphold me and I will be delivered.
Psalm 119:116–117

Chapter 6

The Way We Run

*We do not choose suffering simply because we
are told to, but because the one who tells us to
describes it as the path to everlasting joy.*
—John Piper

After Lazarus has been in the tomb for four days, Martha
received word that Jesus was coming. Jesus halted by the
city gates, and she ran to meet Him there. The first thing we are
told about their conversation is that Martha tells the Lord her
brother would still be alive if He had been there (John 11:21).

Was she blaming Him? Was she angry with Him?

Based on reading several commentaries on this passage, it
seems likely that she wasn't angry but was declaring her faith in
Him. This faith is evidenced by her next statement, "But I know
that *even now* God will give you whatever you ask" (John 11:22).
I can see her face, broken with despair as she clings to the one
possibility that still exists.

If You are who You say You are, it is not too late.

Jesus responded by saying that Lazarus would rise, which Martha misinterpreted as a referral to His resurrection into heaven on the last day. It is easy to jump to the assumption that He is going to intervene but not in the way we want Him to. Flying us all up to heaven somehow seems more likely than raising a dead man from the grave. I love what happens next. He has a way of doing things like this in our lives, doesn't He?

He began by reminding her who He is, "I am the resurrection and the life. He who believes in me will live, even if He dies; and whoever believes in me will never die" (John 11:25, author paraphrase). Then He asked the hard question.

"Do you believe this?"

Ouch.

Not much room for negotiation, is there?

He knew she believed in Him because He knew her heart and her mind. I believe He asks us this question in our lives because sometimes we need to hear our own voices responding to His call. I see more of Martha in myself than I want to admit. I have expectations of Him, and although at my core I know that *He* is God, I am hurt when I feel like He hasn't met me where I wanted Him to be. I have come to many crossroads in my life, and my pregnancy with Audrey was one of the hardest. In these moments we are faced with the question that must be answered as we look deep into the eyes of the Father.

Either He is or He isn't.

There is no middle ground.

He didn't ask her if she was sad or if she was disappointed. He didn't tell her anything more about her brother. He paused, mid-conversation, and asked her where her faith was.

"'Yes, Lord,' she told him, 'I believe that you are the Christ, the Son of God, who was to come into the world'" (John 11:27).

Beautiful, isn't it?

Jesus simply and comfortably showed patience with her questioning and misunderstanding, using it as an opportunity for her to hear her own words of faith. This is Who He is to me, as so many times He has taught me in this same way. My doubt is diffused by the simplicity of His request. Over and over during the days of my pregnancy, I heard my own voice whispering, *"I do believe"* into the great expanse that bridged my personal reality with that declaration.

After she finished her statement, Martha went back to the house where her sister Mary was waiting and said, "The Teacher is here, . . . and is asking for you" (John 11:28). The passage specifies that the message was given to her privately, probably so news of Jesus' presence wouldn't lead to a crowd going to the Lord as well.

Let's take a minute to back away a bit and see the big picture. The Lord had a good reason to maintain privacy because He knows that this journey to Judea is actually the beginning of a series of events that will put His Father's plan for Him in motion. He knows that as soon as He returns to Judea, He will be returning to a place of hostility and hatred where He will soon be beaten and hung to die. He is walking headfirst into the will of His Father.

He is coming to them in order to leave them, and He knows it.

What a walk that must have been, step after agonizing step, all the while knowing what His destination held in store for Him.

So Jesus waited at the entrance of the city, and as soon as Mary heard that He was calling for her, she got up and ran. Of course all of those around her had seen her sister talking to her, and based on her response, they believed she was going to wail at the tomb. They rose and followed Mary through the dusty streets to the place where she greeted her Savior with tears of reverence and desperation.

I love this image. I cling to it, in fact.

Here is a woman who has watched her beloved brother die. Yet, as soon as she hears that Jesus is near, she cannot help but gather up her dress around her and run to Him.

Do you?

I am speaking from experience when I say it doesn't always come naturally. But I also know that every time her feet hit the ground and people turned to see her scurrying past them, her Father was glorified. Every time we take one step closer to Him, we are honoring Him with our faith.

I can see her in my mind's eye; it is a visual that has carried me through moments of tremendous pain. Heart pounding, hair loosened by the wind, face flushed from effort, she keeps her pace until finally she sees Him.

The One Who *can.*

As soon as she reached Jesus, she fell at His feet and asked Him the same question her sister had asked. Knowing what I do about Mary from other portions of Scripture, I believe that while she wanted Him to know she lamented His absence and her brother's death, her actions were a show of unwavering faith. I love the reckless adoration that Mary had for her Lord because it produced an infectious hope in all those who witnessed it. I desperately wanted to be this faith filled and quick to worship despite the burden I was carrying as we prepared for Audrey's birth.

What incredible, inspiring faith, a woman in the wake of loss who can think of nothing more than falling at her Master's feet. Like her sister, Mary expressed her remorse that He hadn't arrived sooner and used the phrase Martha used when speaking to Him, "*Kai nyn.*"

Even now.

I walked into the doctor's office more times than I can count and thought those same words as I waited for an update on my daughter. *Even now*, Lord. I believe You can heal her even now when she is as good as gone to the world.

One of the most difficult days during my pregnancy was when we went to the cemetery to choose a "resting spot" for Audrey.

They try and make it sound so peaceful and lovely, and I wanted to stand up and tell them just to say it like it was, but I resisted. It was like the time we looked at house plans and laughed over the way they described the rooms. The foyer was referred to as the "welcoming area," the family room was the "gathering area," and the tiny nook in the kitchen made for a table was labeled the "morning room."

It wasn't a glamorous house, but it sure sounded like it was. I mean, who wouldn't want to sip coffee in a "morning room"? And didn't it sound nice to say that it was an area for "resting"? I understand why they do that, because death is ugly. Nobody is going to sell plots by saying, "This is where you can bring the dead body of the person you love."

We spoke with a woman in the office for a while, and she suggested that we take a stroll out in the area where we were considering burying Audrey.

A stroll?

Well, by all means, let's. A stroll sounds *lovely*.

And then we'll have crepes.

The whole thing felt completely absurd.

We walked out to the area of the cemetery that is dedicated to infants and children, and as we walked through the grave markers, we wept. We stopped at many of them and prayed for the families who had lost children, many of them the same day they were born. What an atrocious club to join. Audrey was moving inside me, and every time she shifted slightly, the gap between reality and hope narrowed.

As she hiccupped, I stared at the names engraved around me and imagined myself having to come here to visit her.

It couldn't be.

She was alive and well, and this was a place for the dead.

I pointed to a spot silently and then turned and walked to the car. Todd followed, and as the door closed behind him, I screamed. I don't know what I said, nor does it really matter. It wasn't in the words. It was in the air, in the ground, in this place that I hated being. It was my new life.

We went back and spoke to the "consultant" again, and we quickly realized that her intention was to get a big sale. She kept hinting that we really needed to consider buying a family area and we kept deflecting her suggestion. It was enough to manage to do what we were there to do. It takes quite a bit to get me to the point where I speak sharply to someone I don't really know, but the combination of "used car salesperson" tactics and complete disregard for our pain finally pushed me over the edge.

"For clarification," I began quietly, "this entire meeting is hypothetical."

She looked up from her paperwork because a cemetery isn't normally "Plan B."

"We don't know what is going to happen to our daughter, and we aren't buying anything today. Not one plot and not ten. We are trying to understand our options in the event that we need to explore them in the future. God willing, we will not." I was kind but direct.

She set her pen down. I wasn't done.

"We believe in a God who will have the final say. He hasn't said it yet. And if He does, you won't need to talk us into the Cadillac of coffins because quite frankly, she won't be in there."

This was followed by uncomfortable nodding and throat clearing. We reserved a plot, and I picked up my purse and shook her hand. Todd opened the door for me, and we left that ghastly place.

At least we wanted to.

Unfortunately you can't leave a place like that and not take some of it with you.

A few weeks after we chose her "resting spot," I sat up straight in bed in the middle of the night, and Todd awoke to my sobbing next to him.

"Baby, what's wrong?"

"I need to buy her something to wear. She'll be cold, Toddy."

I was gasping for air, envisioning this sweet life inside me being out of my arms with no blanket or warm clothes. I thought it was a silly and not very spiritual thought and I didn't share it for a long time for fear of people's response. I knew her spirit would be with the Lord, but the image was too much to bear.

The next day I found a Web site that specialized in "resting gowns" for babies who were expected to die at birth. I agonized over several of them, feeling the weight of the world on my shoulders. Finally I chose a simple white dress with tiny roses blooming on the sleeves, and with a few clicks of the keyboard, my heart broke all over again.

"Please, Lord," I whispered.

"Let this dress sit in her closet for years to come, reminding us that we once thought she would have to wear it."

The day after we went to the cemetery, I wrote about the experience on my blog. I can still remember everything as if it were yesterday; reading over these words months later still brings me right back to the wet ground and the depth of sorrow that filled me as we waited.

April 1, 2008

We had a hard day yesterday, a day that was marked by decisions that mommies and daddies shouldn't have to make. Usually I wait to post on here at least until I can breathe and control my tears long enough to see the screen as I write, but tonight I am just letting it spill out of me. I need to be transparent before you in this moment because I so covet your prayers during the next several days.

My spirit is unbearably heavy.

This weekend Todd was on the road for one night. I discovered rather quickly that my physical ability to parent is waning. The girls snacked on their Easter baskets for breakfast (I couldn't get up to help). A few minutes later I realized that Kate didn't have a diaper on and I was in too much pain to get to the top of the stairs to get them. There were many people I could have called who would have been there in two minutes, but I just so wanted to be the mommy.

I wanted to make life seem normal for just one morning. I could feel myself crumbling and I went into the family room to try and find my Bible and my little journal. As I sat, I heard Abby and Ellie whispering a few rooms away and I snuck in to hear the conversation.

"Is Mommy sad?" Abby paused for a response from "Ellie the wise."

"Abby, she's just crying again. She's so sad about her baby. We are going to bury Audrey, and that's why she's sad. She just needs to cry a lot and let her face be red, and then it will be fine."

"Well should we stay in here? Do you think she needs "private-cy?""

"Yeah, I think she does. We'll stay here. Then we can check her and see if she's done yet."

Doll playing resumes.

Two five-year-olds having a very grown-up conversation about which shade of pink dress matches the Barbie skating shoes and also the fact that Mommy is basically falling apart in our presence and we need to figure out how to cope with it. Then I noticed my sweet Kate, with chocolate all around her mouth, playing alone at the top of the stairs with her dollies. She had given up on trying to find me. Even if she had been sitting on my lap, she would see that I could not be found. I was not present to care for the girls because I hurt so much in so many ways. This is the hardest part to bear.

I snuck to my spot on the sofa, and I just let the weeping overtake me. The emotion I felt after hearing my daughters' mature approach to such a complicated situation overwhelmed me. I begged God to shelter them from what was happening, to fill their minds with peace. I was so alone, so hurt, so sad. I felt my body just start to shut down with my mind tired and restless. My bones ached and refused to help me stand. When Todd got home not long after, I was a mess. I told him that I just needed to get in my bed for a little while and talk to the Lord. I just needed to force myself into stillness.

I lay down for several hours. I prayed. I slept. I beseeched God. I cried. I accepted His decisions. I begged for Him to change His mind. I became filled with a sorrow that has not been present this entire journey. Just a deep-down, settled sorrow that soaks into every part of you and claims it as its own. I surrendered and fell asleep.

The amount of physical pain I am experiencing is intense. I wanted to know why it was this way, so we called yesterday morning and set up an ultrasound.

When we went in for our appointment, our favorite technician was there, and we all got caught up for a few minutes. I felt like Audrey had shifted because of the pressure I was feeling, and she has. She is now in a frank breech position, which will require a C-section as we had planned. We watched her open and close her mouth and wiggle her little body around. She has shifted from one side of my body to the other, and she is still enjoying the hiccups at least a few times a day.

I want to mention these things here because this is what we know of her. We know she likes to put her hand in her mouth and she doesn't like when she feels things resting on her and getting into her space. We know she has a perfect little nose and that she is tiny, tiny. We know that she likes to move her head in different positions and that she kicks when her daddy sings to her. We know that she is about two and a half pounds and that she doesn't like it when I lie on one side too long. And of course, the beautiful part is that we get to respond to what she likes. She loves peanut butter and jelly so I can eat it and feel her jumping around. We have formed a system within our family of how we are able to love her in the bits we know.

Abby likes to run her hands gently over my belly and ask if she is "hearing" her as she makes shapes with her fingers and whispers secrets to her that I can't even know. Ellie talks to her but doesn't expect a response. I think she feels like the big sister, always working out the details of how things are going to be. She'll say, "You are going to be with Jesus, and that will be so great. We will cry and miss you though." She likes to tidy things up in a bow whereas Abby could get lost choosing the different textures and colors of all the potential bows before she would ever think of tidying. Kate likes to put her toys right on my tummy as if she is waiting for Audrey to jump in and play. She also likes to make animal noises for her, and then she laughs hysterically for both of them.

We are all just doing the best we can, minute by minute, to love our sweet Audrey well. We talk to her all day long. Sometimes I take a bath and tell her all about what swimming is like or what it's like to be on the beach in the hot sun. I tell her about my favorite poets, my favorite memories of childhood, and my love for God and for her daddy.

The two of us have covered much ground in this sacred dance we call pregnancy. I feel bonded to her in a way I never did with my others because I know this is all I have. And yet there is so much I can never give her.

I want her to know that I was funny.

That I would have come at three in the morning if she got scared and needed a ride.

That I would have loved to have heard the sound of her children floating through my house as I got older.

I wanted to try and fit a lifetime of love into a few short months, and as we approach the end of the road, it occurs to me that there isn't enough time to tell her everything. And so now I have to trust a different side of God the Father. Will You tell her all about me and what I would have been to her? Will You show her glimpses of how we would have lived life together?

My heart is breaking because I want her to know that I would have painted her little toenails and taken her to swimming lessons. I didn't want to miss it all. Lord, will You tell her how much she was loved and how much we will always mourn her absence? Lord, please pour Yourself into these hurts as only You can, and we will rest knowing she is safe with You.

After all of the anguish of the past few days, and from what we consider sound medical advice, we have made the decision to move Audrey's due date forward one week. She is now scheduled to be born at 4:00 p.m. on Monday April 7.

We are desperate for peace, for unexpected joy, for as much time with her as God would allow, and for enough grace for the time that He won't.

We long for her. We long to know the next page in this chapter . . . to His glory, whatever it may be.

"Rejoice in the Lord always; again I will say rejoice! Let your gentle spirit be known to all men. The Lord is near. Be anxious for nothing, but in everything by prayer and supplication with thanksgiving let your requests be made known to God. **And the peace of God, which surpasses all comprehension, will guard your hearts and your minds in Christ Jesus"** *(Phil. 4:4–7 NASB, emphasis added).*

Philippians 4:7 has been quoted to us so many times as we have walked this journey. I looked it up today to write down and was struck by the fact that Audrey will be born on 4/7. We trust that this was for us to find refuge in, and we do.

I didn't feel comfortable sharing on my blog about some of the reasons we had chosen to deliver Audrey when we did, but I want to do so here. I feel very vulnerable sharing some of the most intimate details of her situation, but I am trusting that the Lord will use them to minister to others who may be where I was.

One of the basic reasons we chose to have her when we did was that my body was just so tired. Without the benefit of amniotic fluid to cushion her, carrying her had become incredibly uncomfortable. I would have continued on through that, of course, but there were many other variables. Todd was on and off of his tour. We were scared that he would be on the road and I would go into labor and deliver before he could get home. Because I had delivered so quickly in the past, we had to face the reality that he might not be able to meet her alive if that happened. Neither of us could stand that possibility so we decided we needed to schedule the delivery. When we consulted with our doctor, he explained that there was really no reason to wait until I was farther along and that she might pass away before then.

I have never shared this publicly, but the doctors gave scary descriptions of what might happen if I went into labor. Because of her position, she would be delivered in a breech position. She was so fragile that my doctor was concerned she would not be born in one piece. I will never forget his description of this, and the graphic nature of the explanation shook us to the core. The reality was that if she came feet first, there was a possibility, in his words, "that she may not be delivered whole."

I have never been able to shake that image.

I know it is shocking for you to read, but it just wasn't something I was ready to share at the time we were told. Understandably we told him we would not, under any circumstances, allow that to happen. So here I was, a woman who had a history of violent, preterm delivery, and we had to make a decision that we thought would be best for her.

I faced the most difficult request of my life at that point, a question I hope you never have had to answer.

We had to decide the day our daughter would die.

I went home and flipped calendar pages, begging the Lord to guide my fingers.

I circled April 7, 2008 and wrote beside it, "Happy Birthday, Audrey."

Then I lay on the floor of my kitchen and sobbed.

My God, my God, why have you forsaken me?
Why are you so far from saving me?
so far from the words of my groaning?
O my God, I cry out by day, but you do not answer,
by night, and am not silent.
Psalm 22:1–2

For we do not have a high priest who is unable to sympathize with our weaknesses, but we have one who has been tempted in every way, just as we are—yet was without sin. Let us then approach the throne of grace with confidence, so that we may receive mercy and find grace to help us in our time of need.
Hebrews 4:15–16

Chapter 7

The Weeping
and the Wailing

Joy in affliction is rooted in the hope of
resurrection, but our experience of suffering
also deepens the root of that hope.
—John Piper

I wrote the following on April 6, 2008, the night before Audrey's birth, and I didn't dare try to re-create what I was feeling that evening as I worked on this book. It still makes me cry to read because I can remember being perched in my bed while every possible scenario for the next day plagued me. I knew generally what to expect, but there was always room for either a miracle or something unexpectedly worse.

It feels like it was yesterday. I can still remember the smell of the candle that burned on my bedside table as I summoned the strength to pray. I finally fell asleep after watching the light dance around the dark room, and, looking back, I can't help but note the symbolism.

There was still a flicker of light, and I wanted to cling to it.

April 6, 2008

When I was about four years old, I was hospitalized for several days because I battled with overwhelming anxiety. I remember the hospital room, the way I would watch out the door when it was open to see who was coming. They made me draw pictures and ran all kinds of tests. I saw a child psychologist as well, and the best part was that my parents took me out to dinner afterward and I felt very fancy.

At the time I didn't understand that something was wrong with me or that I was different from other kids. My stomach hurt all of the time. I used to make my father walk me around the house before bedtime to make sure that the stove was turned off, the front door was locked, and my baby sister was breathing in her crib. I would worry for hours about things that could happen to my family, to my house, to myself. I vividly remember asking my dad what he would do in the event that someone broke into our house and tried to hurt us. Did he have some kind of plan? Was he strong enough to overtake a burglar if he needed to?

I worried at school. I worried that kids wouldn't like me, that something would happen to my mom while I was away, that my sister would have to eat alone in the cafeteria (I actually broke the rules several times to sneak to the kindergarten side and sit with *her until they would catch me and send me back to the second-graders).*

I just worried. I never wanted anyone to feel like they weren't "taken care of," and for my entire life this pattern has remained constant. When we were at Disney World recently, I walked into a little shop that I remembered from childhood. All the stuffed animals were on the same wall that I had pictured them on in my memories. I got so choked up remembering myself as a little redheaded girl who stood in front of the Goofy dolls (he was my favorite), tenderly lifting one off the shelf and then feeling the overwhelming guilt that all the other ones would be sad because I hadn't chosen them. I would look at their faces and try to decide which was the most needy so that I could rescue him. I vividly remember walking away with the "chosen" one and starting to cry because all the other ones must have felt abandoned.

I refused to come down the stairs on Christmas morning when I was five because I was convinced that Santa didn't find me worthy of toys. I hid under the covers and cried and cried until my dad brought me some red and white pom-poms from under the tree to prove that Santa had come and that he had remembered me. I have always had the feeling that I needed to be the rescuer, that I needed to keep people safe, that I needed to be good enough.

I have never been completely able to shake these emotions. They came with me to college, to graduate school, to marriage, to the delivery room, to the doctor's office. To the ultrasound where I was told that my worst fears had been confirmed. They walk beside me in the daylight and wake me in the night. Fear wraps itself around me and refuses to let go. I can feel my fingers getting numb, my vision getting hazy, my breathing quicken; and I know it is upon me. But I believe now, years later, that this voice has a name, and he lurks in the shadows, waiting to devour. I feel that I have been in the midst of spiritual warfare as I have walked this path, and I have constantly had to silence the enemy with the only word that can. I utter the name of Jesus as I get into bed, as I cry in the night, as I sense the evil that Satan has tempted me to believe.

Today he has sought me out. He is painting horrific images of tomorrow to shake me to the core, to tell me that my Lord has no power to intervene now.

He is telling me it is too late.

I have not made it out of bed today because I have so sensed the need to concentrate wholly on what I know to be true, even when I don't feel it. A few hours ago I talked to God about what I was feeling, and I begged mercy for my doubts. He reminded me gently of a man named Job, whom He loved and knew as a righteous, holy man whose heart was filled with His spirit. He allowed Satan to test Job, to take away what was most precious to him. Job walked through the depths of suffering, more than I can fathom. I opened my Bible to his story and asked God what He wanted from me today, on the eve of the day where I have been called to anticipate the loss of my sweet daughter.

He spoke, as He always does. I wasn't necessarily expecting to hear what He said in that moment, as I wept openly before Him in the profound wake of sadness that surrounds me.

I want you to praise Me.

He didn't ask me to praise Him because He was going to perform a miracle, although He knows that I would. He asked me to praise Him because He will be the same tomorrow regardless of what happens to Audrey. Is that hard for me to wrap my heart around?

Yes.

Does everything in me want to protest letting someone else be in charge?

Yes.

It has been my mode of survival since I was born. My parents told me that moments after I was born, I lifted my head off my mother's body and scanned the room. I was probably making sure someone was going to bring me to the right place and that the doctor was well aware of what he needed to be focusing on in that moment.

I have a history of not letting someone else take care of things. And now I am being called to praise the One who is allowing this season? The One who has taken every bit of control from me?

Seriously?

I sat in silence. I closed my eyes and thought about who He is to me, what He has been to me in the bitterness and in the joy. I felt like He was beside me, waiting. And in that moment I felt myself rest. My mind was still. All I know is that without intending to, I smiled. It was the most ridiculous thing you could ever imagine unless you know what I know. And I hope you do.

He is Lord.

Only He.

Not me, not Todd, not my doctors, not my parents.

He.

We don't know what tomorrow will look like or how it will be remembered ten years from now. We can't begin to imagine the road that lies ahead of us, but I know that I will remember today as being a day that I trusted Him despite the hurt.

I want you to know, especially if you do not know the Lord, that He is real. This is not a fairy-tale, coping mechanism that I rely on when I need to escape from reality. It is not something I do because it's nice to have a place to dress up for on Sunday mornings. It is my fervent prayer that somehow I can manage in this post to find a balance between not alienating people and sharing my heart. It's just that I don't know how people get through things like this without Him. I can barely choose stuffed animals without having a heart attack, and today, because of Christ, I am filled with peace. I pray the same for each of you as you walk through your own life.

One way or another our daughter will be healed tomorrow. Praise God with me tonight for this truth.

I awoke on April 7 with knots in my stomach.

I was finally going to meet my Audrey, and yet the reality was that I was probably going to have to let her go as well.

We got to the hospital around daybreak, and as we parked the car, we saw our pastor arriving at the same time. He came over and hugged each of us, and then we all made the long walk over to the waiting room. It was a quiet walk, with Todd's fingers and mine intertwined and our hearts pounding. Truly there was nothing left to say. We knew what the plan was for the day but later discussed those moments and learned we were thinking the same thing.

We were still holding out for a miracle.

Todd signed me in, and the receptionist looked at me sadly. She nodded her head in recognition of what this day was going to be for me. I smiled back despite the fact that I was having trouble just standing up. We checked into our room, and the memories of my other deliveries haunted me. This was supposed to be a beautiful place of beginnings, and I was overwhelmed by sadness.

Our pastor walked the halls in prayer, intermittently checking in to see how we were holding up. Nurses came in and out, checking equipment and talking to me as the sound of Audrey's heartbeat filled the room.

Eventually it was time.

I was wheeled to an operating room and after a few minutes I remember Todd coming back in with his surgical mask on, eyes peeking over at me with desperate love. I stared at him, remembering the joy that had always been present in this moment in the past. We heard the instruments being opened, and Todd squeezed my hands as one nurse came to my right side and another to my left. They kept their faces nearly touching mine, breathing silent prayers as we waited for word from Dr. T.

"We're starting to cut, Angie. Can you feel that?"

I shook my head no and told my nurse practitioner I felt like I was going to pass out. I was so worried about passing out because I wanted to hold Audrey alive, and I knew I would be devastated if I didn't get the chance. She nodded and must have put something in my IV because I started to feel less dizzy. I could feel pressure and tugging, but it was so quiet.

And finally the moment I had been anticipating was upon us.

"She's out." Our doctor said it boldly, definitively, and the room breathed in the expectation.

Todd repeated the words as if in a dream, and peeked over to see my stomach in the hopes of catching a glimpse of her.

My mind was racing, and I briefly saw her little body being passed to the table nearby as the nurses gathered around her.

I wanted someone to tell me something, anything, but I was terrified to know. I mustered up the courage to ask the burning question that was filling my mind, fearing the worst.

"Is she alive?" I asked it softly, as if I had already been defeated by the answer.

"She's alive, sweetie. And she's beautiful." Todd leaned over me and cried as he kissed me over and over. I was exhausted with relief, and I looked to see what the nurses were saying.

Everything was moving slowly all around me. The noises, the slight movements, the nodding heads and discussion, all just out of reach of my grasp.

Even now, oh Lord, even now.

It felt like forever as the minutes passed. I asked Todd questions as he walked back and forth between his wife and his daughter, trying to understand what was happening. I learned that she had tiny fingers and tiny toes. I heard them say she had sweet, puckered lips.

And red hair just like her mommy.

And she was breathing.

Because we had discussed what was going to happen immediately after she was born, I knew that the nurses wanted to confirm the diagnosis before they made any decisions. They were going to do this as quickly as possible so that if their expectations were correct, they could give her to me right away.

I watched them assess her, and I tried to read their faces as they hovered over my baby girl. I was desperate for a glimpse of hope, and I began to sense something had shifted as they looked her over.

"What are they saying, Toddy?" He walked over to them again, and he said he couldn't really hear them but that she looked really peaceful and she was still breathing well.

Kai nyn, Lord.

It felt like something must be going on because they weren't leaving, and they weren't saying anything to us. We didn't dare ask because we didn't want to break the seal of possibility. I stared at my IV pole, watching the fluid drip as I waited for them to tell us what they were seeing.

I felt like they might have been wrong and that they were going to turn around and tell me that she was okay. She didn't look the way they had anticipated, based on what Todd was telling me, and it was all feeding into my hope.

Her face was flushed with life, arms moving slowly around her, reaching for touch.

My heart was pounding.

She was going to be OK.

It was all a mistake.

I stared at them, staring at her.

And then in one swift movement, it happened.

I saw one nurse lower her stethoscope, followed by three others. They said a few things quietly and then filed out of the room with their heads down.

And just like that, I knew.

She wasn't going to stay.

All the months, all the dreams, all the hopes for a miracle.

Gone.

And I hadn't even seen her yet.

The door closed behind them and they took with them the last shred of possibility. I hadn't even seen her face yet, and as Todd went to bring her to me, I prepared to say hello to my daughter.

It was clear to me after a few soft words from my nurse that I would also need to prepare to say good-bye.

As the doctors worked silently behind the blue curtain draped over me, Todd went to Audrey and picked her up. I saw her tiny form, her bright hair, her fingers reaching out of her blanket.

He laid her on me, face-to-face. Nose to nose. As close to each other as this world allows.

She smelled like unexpected, beautiful life.

I soaked every bit of her in. She had blood on her arms and on her head, and I wiped it off—a first motherly instinct to care for her in the moments I had the chance.

She had one of her eyes open just slightly and a calm expression on her face. I remember talking to her, but I don't recall all of the things I said. I know I told her I loved her. Later one of the nurses in the room told me that she had heard me repeating, "You don't have to stay for us, baby. Jesus will watch you. We'll see you soon. Go to Him if it's time."

She said they hid behind the big blue curtain and cried while Dr. T sewed up the only wound he could.

I can still feel that moment, and I thank the Lord for it. I have never felt the urgency of love the way I did as I cradled her. It was desperate, peace-filled, crazy love.

"Her heart rate is slowing rapidly, Angie. We don't think she has much time. The NICU nurses who were just here confirmed what they needed to, and we all want you to have this time with her."

She choked on her words because she wasn't just a nurse to my family and me. She was a sister in Christ and a friend. With every effort to maintain her professional role, she blinked away her tears and reached down to me.

"I am so sorry." She whispered the only thing she could, and then she turned her head away abruptly, fighting what she knew was going to overtake her, and walked out of sight.

They were finished with the surgery, so they rolled us down the hallway and into the elevator as I held Audrey. We made our way to the labor and delivery floor. As I rolled down the endless hallways, I had to consciously ignore the sounds that came from behind the doors. New mothers with their babies, bundled in goodness and promise while my tear-stained cheek pressed to the one who probably wouldn't see the sun set that night.

But still I was her mommy.

I held her, and despite the tears I showed her off to whoever looked down at me.

"Her name is Audrey." I said to a nurse who didn't know the situation.

"Well, isn't she the most precious thing." She moved her blanket away from her face. "And look at that hair!"

"I know. We're so excited she's here." I smiled and kissed Audrey's warm head.

I wasn't angry. I was strangely, impossibly at peace. If you were to ask me what emotion dominated for the next several hours, I would say it was joy.

I've seen a beautiful quote frequently referenced by various individuals that sums it up perfectly, "Joy is not the absence of trouble but the presence of Christ." I have no doubt that the Lord was in our midst and that He drank deeply of our sorrow that day.

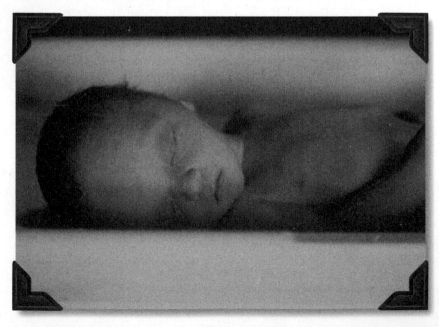

In His infinite mercy He allowed us to embrace the moments we had and to live those hours as if they were going to go on forever.

The tiny hospital room became filled with the voices and prayers of our closest friends and family, and we rejoiced that she was in our arms. As she was passed from person to person, I watched as they all cooed over her and touched her face. It struck me many times that day that if anyone were to walk into that room with no explanation, they wouldn't have known it was any different from a normal celebration of a baby's birth.

I watched the water trickle down her back as Todd gave her a bath and laughed out loud as they announced that she weighed over three pounds. They didn't believe she would weigh that much, and this small victory was a reminder that she had true weight here.

With her smelling fresh and clean, Todd and his mother buttoned the back of her dress carefully and placed a tiny pink bonnet on her head. Abby, Ellie, and Kate climbed up on the bed and marveled at how tiny she was. Kate pulled her close to her chest like a doll and kissed her over and over while Abby played with her toes. My nurse came in periodically to check her heart rate. I had asked her to be very discreet when Audrey left us because I didn't want the girls to be alarmed.

A little more than two hours after she was born, and with all the girls still gathered around me on the bed, the nurse checked her pulse. When she finished, she gently straightened Audrey's gown back into place and nodded at me. I nodded back, and the girls talked to her while I mouthed the words, "She's gone" to Todd.

In that moment the Lord took her from our arms into His.

Right before our eyes, she passed from this world to the next, and all she had ever known was love.

A few minutes later I told the girls that she was with Jesus and that we should be so happy that she was all better. They weren't scared because they were looking at her. I had explained that after she died, her body would just be a shell like a doll baby, but the real Audrey would be in heaven.

It was one of the hardest moments of my life.

I asked Abby if she wanted to play "This Little Piggy" on her tootsies.

She nodded, and we peeled the blanket away from her lifeless feet.

"This little piggy went to market."

She played happily while I closed my eyes and prayed for the Lord to sustain me.

For the strength to accept that the cup had not passed.

For trust in Him despite the fact that I felt horribly, maddeningly betrayed. That is the beauty of His love for His children. Even as our hearts rage within us, He stands, ever present, and embraces our pain.

What did He think of all of this? What God watches a child die in her mother's arms and doesn't intervene? How could any of these things really be happening?

The questions remained as I held her for many more hours. It grew harder during that time because we knew we were approaching the moment where we would have to say good-bye.

We fell asleep with her in our arms, and once everyone had left, Todd and I talked to her and made sure we saw every part of her. Around 4:30 a.m. Todd and I prayed over her, and I called the nurse's station and told them we were ready.

We weren't, of course, but we sensed that it was time. I wanted to remember her just the way she was, and the signs of death were beginning to catch up with her. They had warned me beforehand that it was probably not in out best interest to keep her twelve or so hours after she passed so that we wouldn't be subject to watching her body change. As the hour approached, we prepared to give her away.

I clung to her, staring at the door, keenly aware a part of me was going to go with her, never to return.

She was cold, heavy with the sting of mortality.

I wrapped her blanket tighter.

I knew it couldn't warm her, but it was the only thing that made sense. I made sure her dress was on underneath, and as I bundled her up, I lowered my face to hers for the last time and told her what was going to be happening. I knew she wasn't there anymore, but the mother's heart doesn't know how to stop loving, even in the wake of death.

A shard of light filled the dark room as the door opened, and my eyes struggled to adjust as a nurse walked in. She walked to my bedside, and I made sure Audrey's feet stayed in her cozy blanket. I lifted her up and into the stranger's arms. The woman never said a word, but her spirit was gentle and loving. We caught eyes for a moment before she turned away.

Then I watched as she took several steps, walked through the doorway with my Audrey in her arms, and closed the door quietly behind her.

As the light of the hallway left our room, we huddled in the darkness and wept over the baby we would never see in this life again.

It was everything I could do not to jump from the bed and, like a woman possessed, chase through the hospital and find her. I stared at the buttons on the bed rail, my last chance to tell them I wanted her back. I restrained myself from calling the nurses and telling them I had made a mistake because I knew it would only postpone the inevitable. All the screams in the world wouldn't change it. Total defeat settled in as Todd lay next to me and we shook with sadness.

Gone.

I had a five-inch long scar that told the world she was mine. And she was gone.

Where was He?

As Mary ran to Jesus and fell at His feet, she was crying (John 11:32). The emotion that Christ feels at this moment is not fully communicated in most modern translations, but the original Greek words are *embrimaomai*, which refers to anger, and *etaraxen heauton*, which means "troubled Himself." One commentary I love said that a better translation of this moment would be that He "became angry in spirit and very agitated."[1]

Many scholars suggest that this emotion was not aimed at the women and men who were gathered around Him but rather at *death itself*. He was angry at the hurt it was causing, and I believe that on that fateful day with my daughter, He was angry that death stole her from us. What happens next in this passage brings tears to my eyes as I think of the way we offered our daughter to Him. Jesus asks where Lazarus is buried, and when the women begin to walk Him to the tomb, Scripture says He weeps (John 11:34–35).

Jesus wept.

Surely these two words are some of the most powerful in all of Scripture, as they reveal the man within deity.

I want to share a beautiful distinction I came upon months after Audrey's death as I poured over these verses. At first glance it appears that Jesus, Mary, and Martha were sobbing together, but the original language of the text reveals that while Jesus was weeping (*dakryo*), the women were wailing (*klaio*). While Mary and Martha were crying out in agony over the loss of their brother, their tears moved Jesus, and He began to weep. This is the only occurrence of *dakryo* in the entire New Testament. He isn't crying over the death of Lazarus but rather the hurt He is experiencing with people He loves dearly. He isn't crying because the situation is hopeless, but because He is an empathetic God.

He knows that in a few moments Lazarus will walk out of the tomb.

He also knows they can't see that hope.

And neither can we.

There is a difference in despair and deep sadness over the time that will pass until we can see her again. It is a conscious, daily choice to experience *dakyro*, the sadness that allows one to grieve with the expectation of redemption.

I stood in the dressing room, staring at the latest in a string of dresses I had decided to dislike. One of the women who had been helping me came to the door and asked how I was doing. She was peppy because it was her job to be.

"I'm doing OK, thank you. I'm just not sure about this." I opened the door and lifted my face so that I was eye to eye with her.

She scanned me, taking a mental inventory of what she had seen in the last twenty minutes. She was adorable, and I guessed her to be about my age. You wouldn't have known it, though. She was radiant with life, while I felt like an old woman playing dress-up. I couldn't remember the last time I wore heels, and I was less than graceful in them.

"You look beautiful! I love that one on you. I think it's my favorite." She clapped her hands together victoriously and asked me about accessories.

I hated to ruin the party, but I had a feeling the balloons were about to pop.

"I think simple would be good. Not showy, just simple." I lifted my fingers slowly to my neckline, absentmindedly sketching where it should fall.

She nodded.

"What's the occasion, sweetie?"

There was no way not to blindside her.

"I'm going to wear it to bury my daughter in a few days."

I tried to say more, but her sweet eyes had covered over with grief, and I knew I didn't need to. She covered her mouth and steadied herself against the door. She hugged me, apologized, and left, unsure what else to do.

Me?

I sat on the floor in my beautiful dress and cried.

When I finally came out, she was waiting for me with a pair of earrings. I stood in front of the mirror as she slipped them gently into my ears. Her hands felt like a mother's, and I stood still until she was finished. She stepped back, and we both took stock of the final product.

"It's a beautiful dress for the ugliest of days," I said. She was crying, but she didn't want me to notice.

I did, and it mattered.

I thanked her for her kindness, and she gathered up my things to take to the register.

A few minutes later I had three new friends, an empire-waisted dress to cover my stomach, and the perfect pearls for a funeral.

The day of Audrey's burial is burned into my mind for many reasons, not the least of which was the fact that the weather was perfect. I had prayed for it to be a beautiful day, and as I slipped into my shoes, I looked out the bathroom window and thanked the Lord for the cloudless sky.

A tent was set up over Audrey's grave site, and people were gathered around her as we pulled up. I didn't want to get out of the car, but I had to.

I remember the feeling of absolute panic and shock when I saw her little coffin. We requested a wooden coffin because they are so simple, and we wanted something that looked like it had been carved by human hands. I originally wanted an Amish coffin, but our funeral home told us that they had a Jewish one that was wooden, and I thought it was beautiful. All of the pictures were of regular-sized coffins, as were all of the displays at the funeral home. I guess my brain didn't fully understand that hers would be a very tiny version of the ones I was seeing. When I first saw it, I gasped out loud.

It was small.

I had to remind myself that she was small too.

It was everything I could do not to run.

When we got closer, I saw my niece peering deep into the hole that had been carved for Audrey. She was standing on the edge of it, leaning her body as far over as she could safely hold herself, staring into the abyss of death. She was curious about it, and I remember thinking that she was the bravest of the bunch.

There was a nice, steady breeze. It was a warm day, and it felt like grace itself was winding its way through the tent as our pastor spoke powerful words of truth. My hair blew all around me, and it reminded me that we are not alone.

We are never alone.

There are wind chimes in the baby garden where she is buried, and there is almost always enough of a breeze to make them dance with music. I remember thinking that the wind was like the Holy Spirit, unseen in this moment but moving.

Ever moving.

At one point Todd's sister Nicol stood to
sing "Be Still My Soul" as she rocked her newborn son Luke.
She swayed like a mother does as she belted through the tears.
I tried not to stare too hard at him cuddled in her arms. She and my
other sister-in-law had been so sensitive and loving with me while
our pregnancies and subsequent deliveries overlapped. Luke was
born a few weeks before Audrey, but they lived out of state so we
had just met him a few days prior. I caught myself moving gently
as if I was rocking my own daughter, but my arms were empty. My
body couldn't accept it any more than my heart could.

We listened as our family members stood and read Scripture
verses over her casket. Then we sang as a family, praise defying
the moment, raised up to the Lord who held her.

Before we ended the service, we had Abby, Ellie, and Kate
come to the casket where we had placed our sweet Audrey Bunny
stuffed animal. We explained that even though Audrey's body was
in the box, her spirit was in heaven, and she was healed. We told

them she didn't need the Band-Aids anymore, and that it was time to take them off.

Kate reached over while Abby and Ellie watched her, and we could hear whispered prayers and sobbing filling the tent. I had imagined that it would be tender and gentle when we removed the dirty, months-old bandages, but it wasn't. She yanked at them purposefully, and when they were off, she threw them into the wind, never to be seen again.

She looked satisfied, and as we all stared at the black mark on the bunny's chest, Ellie patted her head and said, "All better, baby. All better now."

We picked up the bunny, and I told my best friend Audra that I needed to leave before they put Audrey in the ground. I didn't want the kids to see it, so we had decided beforehand that she would drive us home so that Todd could stay and help bury her.

We started the walk to the car, and I heard the sound that haunts me to this day. It was the sound of dirt, hitting the top of the casket, and it was unbearable.

Thump.

No first birthday cake.

Thump.

No sand castles by the water.

Thump.

No sitting up late eating popcorn and watching old movies.

Thump.

Oh, Jesus, be near me now.

I quickened my step to get away from it, but Abby was tugging at my dress and crying so I stopped.

"Mommy, please, can we stay?"

She was really upset and didn't understand why I wanted to leave.

"Honey, we are just going to go home while Daddy finishes things up here, and then they will all come back to our house, so you don't need to be sad about leaving."

She dug her heels into the ground and shook her head, tears spilling onto her long white dress.

"No, Mama. Please no. Please no."

Their cousins are their best friends and I assumed she was disappointed that we weren't staying with them. She continued to protest, so I picked her up and laid her head on my shoulder, trying to shield her from the shovels and the sound of finality.

Audra helped me buckle them in and she started the car, but before we could move, Abby became hysterical. It was so unlike her to react that way. She was kicking the seat, begging us to stop and watch.

"I want to see it, Mommy. Please don't go yet; please don't go yet." She was intent on staring out the window, and from where we were, she could see what they were doing. Audra looked at me to see what I wanted her to do, as I nodded my head to put it back into park.

Audra held my hand as I stared straight ahead, anywhere but there.

After just a few minutes Abby settled down and actually became very peaceful.

With a deep, relieved breath, she said, "OK. We can go ahead now."

I was as perplexed as I was worried because this had been the one thing I didn't want them to remember seeing. I prayed the whole way home that it wouldn't scar them and that I had done the right thing.

When we got home, Audra took the girls outside, and I went up to my bathroom. I sat on the cold tile and cried until I was weak. Todd got home a bit later and asked me what he could do. I told him I wanted to clean the bathroom floor.

He didn't seem confused by my request and went downstairs to get some sponges and cleaner. When he came back up, he handed one to me and kept the other. I wore my silk dress, and he wore his suit. For the next half hour, we were on our knees, scrubbing away the hurt while the smell of fresh soap filled the room.

We ignored the sounds of conversation that came from downstairs, and we hid there until we couldn't hide anymore. I handed him my sponge, surveyed our progress, and smoothed my hair calmly. Hand in hand, we braced ourselves for the beginning of the life where Audrey was unreachable.

Later that night I went to tuck Abby into bed. Her covers were piled so high I could barely see her eyes.

"Abby?"

"What, Momma?"

"Honey, I want to talk about today and about how you're feeling." She poked her head out so I could see her mouth.

"I'm feeling OK." She was tentative, not wanting to worry me.

"You really wanted to stay, didn't you?" She nodded yes, and then her face crumpled in hurt.

I hugged her and after a few minutes she pulled away a bit and looked at me.

"I didn't want it to rain on her, Mommy."

It had never crossed my mind that her seeing the casket go into the ground would be comforting. She wanted to make sure that Audrey was safe, and it made perfect sense.

Well, as much sense as it could.

She curled up on my lap, and I rocked her to sleep.

After she started breathing deeper, I let myself cry. I rubbed her head, brushing the hair out of her face, all the while praying that we would learn how to do this new dance together.

---

1. George R. Beasley-Murray, *John: Word Biblical Commentary Vol. 36* (Waco, TX: Word, 1988), 1982–83.

Your wrath has swept over me;
your terrors have destroyed me.
All day long they surround me like a flood;
they have completely engulfed me.
You have taken my companions and loved ones from
me; the darkness is my closest friend.
Psalm 88:16–18

When you pass through the waters,
I will be with you;
and when you pass through the rivers,
they will not sweep over you.
When you walk though the fire,
you will not be burned;
the flames will not set you ablaze.
For I am the Lord, your God,
the Holy One of Israel, your Savior.
Isaiah 43:2–3

Chapter 8
Cherry Blossom

I thought that prattling boys and girls
would fill this empty room.
That my rich heart would gather flowers
from childhood's opening bloom.
One child and two graves are mine,
this is God's gift to me;
a bleeding, fainting, broken heart,
this is my gift to thee.
—Elizabeth Prentiss[1]

I grew up in Kobe, Japan, and every year we would welcome the cherry blossom festivals with a combination of wonder and sadness. It was the most intensely beautiful time of the year, but it passed so quickly that you felt like you hadn't gotten your fill of the wonder before it was gone. In fact, the Japanese government had to issue an official statement of apology to the Japanese people several years ago when they slightly miscalculated the dates and caused travelers everywhere to miss the peak of the season. It was an incredible sight to see grown men and women running out of their office buildings (which NEVER happens in Japan) and sitting for hours, watching the blossoms float past them in the breeze. My sister and I would dance in them and laugh our heads off because it was the closest thing to perfection we could imagine.

Then it was gone.

All that laid around us were the blossom pieces, reminding us what we had for such a short time. For a while we would pick those up and throw them in the air, but it wasn't the same. The best of it was gone too quickly.

Shortly after Audrey was born, some of my close friends came to my house and told me they had a surprise for us. About half an hour later, they had planted a cherry blossom tree in our front yard in place of one that had not lived. To see those little pink flowers in the place where we had become accustomed to seeing dead branches was profound for me. Several times a day I walk by my dining room windows and smile at the blossoms because they remind me of my past, and they urge me to believe that new life has begun. The soil is rich in longing, needy for purpose, and prepared to be the giver of life. The friends who brought me that tree could not have known the full extent of how meaningful it was to me.

The official name of the tree is the "Yoshino Cherry." Unbeknownst to them, I have always loved Japanese cherry trees and all they remind me of from when they would bloom in Japan. It's not just any cherry tree that is so significant to me, so after the gift from my friends, I did some research to learn more about this special type of cherry tree. What I discovered floored me:

> The Japanese cherry starts flowering profusely from the first warmer days in April, heralding the coming of spring. *The intense beauty and short survival span* have associated cherry blossoms with spiritual and philosophical ideas (such as the beauty and fragility of human life).[2]

I read these words, and I just fell apart. It's OK. I needed to fall apart. I pictured the God of the universe watching two little girls dance under the cherry blossoms in a country so far from home. It was innocence in motion. And here we were, years later, watching my dear friends plant life in a season of loss. Once again, in a small thing I was reminded that none of this is a surprise to Him. Yet there was still more.

As I was researching Japanese cherry trees, I went to a tourism Web site to track the cherry blossom festivals for 2008. I clicked on Kobe. It is this city where so many of my childhood memories come from and fill me with so much joy. I watched the dates come up, and the tears just started falling as I read.

April 7, 2008 . . . one of the peak bloom days.

The day the beauty came and went.

People constantly ask how it is that I am not angry with the Lord. My honest answer is that I have been angry, and I have been disappointed. What I have not been, and what I refuse to be, is disbelieving.

However easy it may be to allow myself to wail over my loss, it is a far more satisfying thing to believe that all of this is a brief season. The Lord I have placed my trust in tells me that I will see my child again, and while He stands beside me, He weeps. He doesn't weep at the barren ground, nor does He mourn the browning branches. He cries because I can't see what He can. And in the fluttering of the breeze, with my heart pressed to His, I can hear Him whisper, *"Spring will come, my love."*

As Mary and Martha cried, those who had gathered around them began to express their doubt. They couldn't seem to get past the belief that if Jesus were God He would have healed Lazarus. They discussed the fact that He had healed others, and it seems they were challenging His claims.

It is easy to be a believer when He gives you a miracle.

People want to know what's so great about a God who would let such awful things happen. How can you put your full dependence on someone who couldn't save your daughter?

What may seem to be unbelief on the part of those who were gathered around Mary and Martha is actually better understood as confusion. Rather than questioning whether or not He *could* heal, they were expressing their curiosity about why He *didn't*.

It's a fair question.

Just today Todd and I ran into a man who hadn't seen Todd for years and he told him that his daughter was miraculously healed. It is human nature to wonder why God cures some and lets others die. All kinds of smart people can probably give you text-book answers, but for those of you who are reading this, I want to offer a perspective that might make more sense to you.

I have no idea.

I have to be honest about this because as a woman with a swollen belly and empty cradle, I didn't really want to hear the big philosophical explanations. I didn't want to hear people try to tell me that it was for the best because, quite frankly, I didn't feel that way. I know that people want to help, but there is a safe place with the Lord where we don't have to have all of the answers.

As Christians, we often want to tie it up neatly with a bow and be standing ready with our church smiles when someone asks us how we are dealing with loss. I don't believe that "God needed another angel," and I honestly grew weary of hearing people try to explain it all away because they couldn't stand to say those three words.

I don't know.

I know there are people reading who are where I was, and I don't want you to think that you need to have answers. Your God is perfectly capable of revealing Himself. You don't have to feel like you need to fill the gaps. He has put the gaps there so that you will press into Him despite them. *That* will be your answer to those who murmur around you.

Soon after Audrey's diagnosis, we were comforted by a story found in 2 Samuel 12. The passage chronicles the events of the day that King David finds out that his infant son has died. He had been desperately pleading to the Lord to spare his son's life. He had fasted and refused to eat as he wept and pled. After his son

died, his servants were afraid to tell him what had happened, yet
David sensed that his son had died.

> *David noticed that his servants were whispering*
> *among themselves and he realized the child was dead.*
> *"Is the child dead?" he asked.*
>
> *"Yes," they replied, "he is dead."*
>
> *Then David got up from the ground. After he had*
> *washed, put on lotions and changed his clothes, he*
> *went into the house of the LORD and worshiped. Then*
> *he went to his own house, and at his request they*
> *served him food, and he ate.*
>
> *His servants asked him, "Why are you acting this*
> *way? While the child was alive, you fasted and wept,*
> *but now that the child is dead, you get up and eat!"*
>
> *He answered, "While the child was still alive, I fasted*
> *and wept. I thought, 'Who knows? The LORD may be*
> *gracious to me and let the child live.' But now that he*
> *is dead, why should I fast? Can I bring him back*
> *again? I will go to him, but he will not return to me."*
> *(2 Sam. 12:19–23)*

She will not return to me.

Six words that will shape every one of my remaining days on
Earth.

It was a season that was cut short, and we continue to grieve the
loss of what she would have been. Yet we also believe that David's
words bring unspeakable hope and remind us that we do not wait
in vain. No, she will not come back to us. But the Lord has gifted
us with the rest of the story. His Word is water to our thirsty souls,
and we drink deep of the promise He has made to us. If you have
walked the valley of grief, or are walking it right now, I want you
to know that I don't have the answers.

I wholly believe that He is real and that He is in control.

I believe He is working everything in my life, and yours, for good.

I believe He *can*.

But if He didn't?

I stand beside you in spirit, weeping, and I pray for the promise of eternity to be carved deeply, unmistakably, into the very fiber of your hurt. Do you believe that the Lord is who He says He is and that He has accomplished what He says He has accomplished? If you do, then know that you are walking a road that leads to Him and to your precious lost children.

No, they will not return to us.

But one day, not so far from now, we will go to them.

---

1. A woman who has greatly helped me as I processed this tremendous loss is Mrs. Elizabeth Prentiss, who lived from 1818–1878. She was a remarkable woman who suffered unbearable loss twice in the same year. She lost her son Eddy at the age of four in 1852. Just a few months later, her newborn daughter also died. Scribbled on a piece of paper, a brief poem with a breathtaking perspective was discovered after her passing. This poem was then published in *101 More Hymn Stories* by Kenneth W. Osbeck (Grand Rapids, MI: Kregel, 1985), 185.

2. FlowerExpert Online, "Japanese Cherry," see http://www.theflowerexpert.com/content/mostpopularflowers/morepopularflowers/cherry-blossom.

Has God forgotten to be merciful?
Psalm 77:9

Therefore we do not lose heart. Though outwardly
we are wasting away, yet inwardly we are being renewed
day by day. For our light and momentary troubles are
achieving for us an eternal glory that far outweighs them all.
So we fix our eyes not on what is seen, but on what is unseen.
For what is seen is temporary, but what is unseen is eternal.
2 Corinthians 4:16–18

Chapter 9
The Stone We Move

Yet she kept discovering in the places of deepest
aloneness and emptiness the God who was with
her, for her. She discovered Christ's presence from
the inside out, seeing what He sees as He sees it.
She now has a sense of what the world looks
like from a cross. She knows the darkness of
the inside of a grave. And she knows, more and
more, the brightness of a new day when the
world is glimpsed as from a tomb, its stone rolled
away. —Mark Buchanan

Jesus could have healed Lazarus without even coming to Bethany. He chose to resurrect him the way He did for the benefit of those who saw it. It's the same today. Have you ever felt like you have been invited to be a part of His miracle? As Jesus, Mary, and Martha arrive at the tomb, He asks those present to move the stone that is blocking the entrance. Instead of running to it in obedience, Martha questions him, telling Him that the stench of decomposition would be too strong.

It sounds ridiculous to be worried about something as silly as a smell when there might be a chance to see your brother again, but this is much more powerful than Martha's words.

It is not about the stench. It is about trust.

He asked them, and He asks us, to be a part of the miracle. How do we respond to this? Are we so distraught over our perceived fears and disappointments that we are paralyzed, or do we trust Him enough to put our hands on the rock? There is no middle ground. Those are our two options: fear or trust.

Throughout my pregnancy with Audrey, the Lord enabled us to move the stone. In every doctor's appointment, every prayer-bathed decision, every time we felt her kick, and every breath we took, He invited us to believe. We all have some Martha in us, so it is easy to focus on the potential problems with what we feel the Lord leading us to do, but that is exactly why He does it.

> Jesus would ask us: "Do you believe? Do you trust? Do you trust that God loves you so much that he wants to give you only life?" When I try to answer, I realize how far I have to go. Much in me says, "I want to be sure that there are certain things in place before I take a leap of faith." Every time I try to trust, I realize how many little conditions I put on trust. Every time I trust more I see how deep is my resistance. And on how many levels I find that faith has not penetrated! We don't know how many levels there are. But our lives are renewed every time we trust more. . . . Indeed, hope born of faith becomes matured and purified through difficulty.[1]

I would love to say I always followed His requests, but I haven't. Many times I stood, hands behind my back, explaining all the reasons I was not moving. After all, what could be worse than walking in front of everyone, mustering up all of my strength, and being let down? Sometimes staying put just feels easier, where there's no more room for disappointment.

Of course, we also may never see what's on the other side of the stone.

Jesus addressed this in His reply to Martha's objection over His request to remove the stone, "Did I not tell you that if you believed, you would see the glory of God?" (John 11:40).

Jesus isn't saying that her faith enables Him to perform the miracle but rather that it allows her to *see* the glory of God. I want to love Him this way. We didn't see Audrey walk out, wrapped in linen, miraculously unharmed. We *did* put our hands on the rock, and when He said, "Push," I can tell you that we did so without hesitation. We stared deep into the cavern of the tomb, anticipating that we might get to see her after all.

I love this part of the story because as we walk through trials, He invites us to trust Him. We aren't guaranteed anything as Christians as far as the outcome, but we are loved enough to be a part of the greatest story ever written. To imagine the same God whose hands marked out the world is allowing us to enter into His plan is profound and humbling. What we are called to do (and I say this with full *belief* but less *earthly comprehension*) is to agree to move the stone, no matter what happens next.

Less than a month after we stood outside the tomb praying our sweet Audrey would emerge, we were still reeling from the fact that she hadn't. I had to face that fact tangibly one rainy day as I braved my way to her grave for the first time.

May 3, 2008

This has been a hard week.

Just six words, but they pretty much sum it up.

After crying through basically every human interaction I have had for the last several days, I realized something in me that needed to be broken. Something that I hadn't felt completely yet. Todd left to go on the road on Wednesday night, and I sobbed like a baby. Shaking, gasping, "Why can't you be an accountant and work 9 to 5?" tears. I was not ready to be alone with my thoughts yet. I wasn't ready to be in charge of the kids, of the house, of anything that did not involve Kleenex. As he left the house around 11:30 p.m., I curled up in my bed, and I invited the sorrow in. She came swiftly, deeply, consumingly. And she whispered to me in the dark of night.

I am here to stay.

We had a rainstorm yesterday (go figure), and I made up my mind that I needed to be with my daughter for a while. As soon as it started to let up, I called my dad, and he came to watch the kids so that I could go to the cemetery. I have wanted to go to her many times before, but I haven't had the strength to be weak.

As I walked through the tombstones in the direction of Audrey's grave, I started to panic. I was alone, and the grass was wet on my toes. What is this new life?

I realized as I wandered that it all looked so different from the day she was buried. There was no white tent. There were no benches. No landmark to find my child. I wandered in and out of headstones, searching and crying. I got myself together enough to try and remember the little map they had given us when we chose her burial spot, and I walked in that direction. I had taken no more than a few steps when I saw the red clay in front of me.

New earth, carving out a spot no more than a foot and a half by two feet.

For a brief moment I regretted my decision. It was too soon.

The grass was still wet from the storm.

The clay was still fresh.

I sat down, not minding that my pants became soaked through or that someone might see me sobbing hysterically. I sat next to her, and I cried until my bones ached and goose bumps covered my legs. I have never in my life felt so lonely. I remembered one of the first things Abby said after she met Audrey. She took a long look at her, and then she asked me quietly, "Do we have to dig now, Mommy?" Just a little girl trying to understand what comes next, and here I was, touching the other side of it already.

I had brought my Bible with me, and I read her a few psalms. All of the ones that God directed me to were about praising the Lord with every breath. I told Him I was pretty sure I had just missed a couple. As I read out loud, the sound of my voice started to fill the void. I stayed that way for about an hour, reading and praying over my baby.

I know she isn't really in there; it's just that her knees are, and I would have loved to kiss them after she fell. I need to mourn the loss of the arms that cannot wrap around me here. Braided hair, a wedding dress, her first wiggly tooth. They are deep within the ground, never to be mine. I needed to feel that loss, and I did.

I do.

I went upstairs to change clothes when I got home, and I caught a glimpse of myself in the mirror. Mascara smudged under my eyes, messy hair, wet clothes. But that wasn't what I saw first. What I saw was the unmistakable patch of rust on my forehead.

Clay.

I must have gotten it on myself somehow while I sat with her. I reached for the towel, and just as I began to wipe it away, a voice reminded me of what I know to be true.

I am here to stay.

I will permanently bear the mark of a woman who has lost her child. Many of us are walking here—in the grocery store, at the neighborhood barbeque, at the movies. We walk without necessarily recognizing each other, side by side and a million miles apart.

If you are one of these women, I want you to know that as I write these words, I am praying for you. I am mourning what you have lost in this life. I am praying that God will fill you as only He can, and that in time, you (and I) will be with our daughters and our sons again.

So what are we to do when we feel the Lord has failed us? We have done every bit of what we felt we could. We trusted Him. We called on Him. We awaited His appearance and even fought doubt as the days passed because above all else, He is good . . . right?

Then He arrived and there was hope. Maybe we even got caught up in the fact that our hands were on the rock that God was going to use to show us His glory. I was there and I believed.

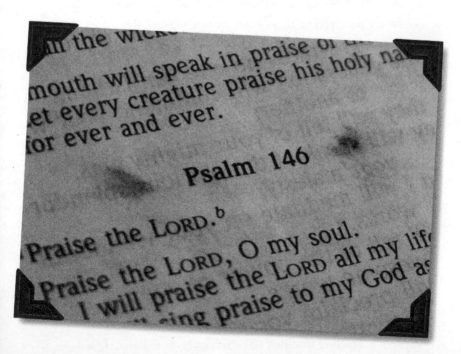

And she remained in the tomb.

I would have stood there forever, longing for Him to rescue me from the reality because feeling so let down was horrible. I know this is a touchy subject for Christians because we are called to trust Him despite what we are experiencing, but if you have been there, you understand.

I want you to imagine the place where you feel the most abandoned by God. Maybe you suffered at the hands of an abuser, or you have painful childhood memories. You may be dealing with a strained relationship or a career misstep. Where is the wound that has ripped into your faith in Jesus?

As hard as this is, I want you to hold that image in your mind and picture the solution, whatever it may be, just on the other side of a stone. Reconciliation? Recovery? Belief where you have none? Redemption where there is only brokenness?

You have waited and waited for this moment and now you are leaning with full weight and eager expectation as the crowd looks on. Now I want you to answer this question honestly.

What do you believe your God can do?

If you had asked me that question right after I lost Audrey, I would have stumbled over my answer. His power is never too small for everyone else, it seems; but when it's me, it feels intangible and unlikely. Even Martha hesitated to be part of what He was doing because she didn't really understand what was about to happen. She might have even been humiliated if it failed as the crowd waited to see what her great Savior was going to do.

I can relate. Sometimes in this world we make fools of ourselves by believing that He is who He says He is.

I felt that. I remember sitting near Audrey's grave, weeds tangling through her grave marker, feeling like I had been made a fool of for trying to move that stupid stone. If I had just accepted that science was science, I wouldn't have let myself believe the way I did. Maybe I wouldn't have felt so hurt and abandoned.

I'm sure that you can think of areas in life where you feel let down by God, even things that have pushed you away from relationship with Him. I won't say I don't understand the questioning because quite frankly it makes all the human sense in the world. What kind of God watches a mother hold her dying baby?

Would you allow me to enter into your heart a bit here?

I believe that everything that happens in our lives, however awful, is an opportunity to bring glory to Jesus. Have I wished it had been in a different way? Of course I do. And you probably do too. If I choose to, I can hold that against Him. I can let it embitter me for the rest of my days, as I walk around finding holes in everything He has done. All of us will have times of crisis. The most we can do is put our hands on the stone and accept what happens next with the grace that says circumstances will define neither God's love for us nor our love for God.

Speaking of the role loss plays in our future, Sue Monk Kidd makes the following observation, "A crisis is a holy summons to cross a threshold. It involves both a leaving behind and a stepping toward, a separation and an opportunity. The word *crisis* derives from the Greek words *krises* and *krino*, which mean,'a separating.'"[2]

In my mind the threshold is what glorifies the Lord. Instead of spending your days focusing on your sense of hurt or loss, allow the Lord to bless you with the grace to believe that what lies ahead will glorify Him. It is the closest thing to true worship that we have in this life, and so often we miss it. I miss it.

It's time to press our full weight into the stone, having complete faith that whether or not there is life in the tomb, there is breath in our lungs to tell of the great Savior who loves us more than we can know.

1. Henri Nouwen, *Turn My Mourning Into Dancing: Finding Hope in Hard Times* (Nashville, TN: Thomas Nelson, 2001), 52–53.

2. Sue Monk Kidd, *When the Heart Waits* (New York, NY: Harper, 1990), 87.

He has made my skin and my flesh grow old
and has broken my bones.
He has besieged me and surrounded me
with bitterness and hardship.
He has made me dwell in darkness
like those long dead.
Lamentations 3:4–6

Trust in the LORD with all your heart
and lean not on your own
understanding;
in all your ways acknowledge him,
and he will make your paths straight.
Proverbs 3:5–6

Chapter 10
Alabaster

Good-night! good-night! as we so oft have said
Beneath this roof at midnight, in the days
That are no more, and shall no more return.
Thou hast but taken up thy lamp and gone to bed;
I stay a little longer, as one stays
To cover up the embers that still burn.
—Henry Wadsworth Longfellow

Years ago a pastor at the church we were attending gave a message about what happened after the resurrection of Lazarus. His sermon contained some of the most profound and moving thoughts I have ever heard about the story of Christ.

Days after his resurrection a celebration was held in honor of Jesus. Everyone was gathered around the Lord when Mary shattered a bottle of perfume and wiped the lavish scent across His feet with her hair. The scent was to be used in a society where bathing was not frequent, so this particular nard was extremely pungent. A few drops would have been more than enough, but without regard to cost or what those around her might think, she simply poured it all out as an act of pure worship. Many have speculated that Mary was preparing her beloved Savior for His death and burial, but our pastor went on to explain that *the scent of the perfume surely would have been on His skin a few days later when He was beaten and crucified. So, in essence, every time a Roman soldier's whip hit Him, the scent of Mary's worship was released and rose all around Him; a reminder of Who He was.*

Wow.

Come with me for a moment to the feast where dozens are gathered around this mysterious, glorious Jesus. As the celebration roars around Him, many people seem to be oblivious to what lies ahead. Whether or not Mary knew what the next several days would entail, we do not know. What we do know is that she could think of nothing in that moment other than an act of absolute devotion and worship.

In the midst of a room full of people, she went to the feet of Jesus. This may not seem like a noteworthy event, but for many reasons it was. Not the least of which was the fact that it was not considered culturally appropriate for her to be sitting at His feet. In addition, Jewish women were not to take their hair down in public. Biblical scholars have suggested that this was her way of acknowledging unworthiness before the Lord.

While Martha was busy serving the guests, Mary pulled the pins out, hair tumbling around her, and bowed low to her Savior. I must admit, I am typically either busy doing what Martha was doing, fretting over everything being just right, or I am paying attention to the rules. It occurred to me how rarely I ignore everything that demands my attention, everything that tells me how I should act, and sit in pure love with eyes only for Him. What a glorious image.

I don't believe her action was simply a reflection of her gratitude over the life of Lazarus because the setting and way the events unfold communicate an inherent heaviness as she pours the perfume. It doesn't feel totally celebratory to me. It feels like letting go.

Regardless of whether or not He had saved her brother, she would have worshipped Him. She loved Him because of Who He was to her, not what He had done for her. She had put her full trust in Him, and that is why she spilled the bottle at His feet. Despite the criticism she received, the Lord recognized what she was doing and commended her. Nothing in this world is of any value unless it is given freely and with abandon to Him, just as Mary's offering was given.

Would I have given every bit of what I had to Him, or would I have thought the way the world did? Many times in life, especially during a season of loss, we are tempted to hold tight to that which has earthly value. The alternative is to know the One who sits before us awaiting our lavish worship, but how difficult that is in the wake of loss.

I still struggle with my false sense of control. In the weeks and months that followed Audrey's death, I could feel my fingers tighten around the bottle He was asking me to pour out. My three daughters, my husband, my house, my parents—everything I could physically put my hands on—felt dangerously out of control. I watched the girls like a hawk, nervous over every movement they made. I went into their rooms at night and watched them while they slept, watching their chests rise and fall.

If you have been through this, you will know that what I am about to say is true.

It never brings relief.

The more we try to cling to our babies, our jobs, our bank accounts, the more we realize that they are not ours. It took me many sleepless nights to be able to walk out of the room, and even now I struggle. As I touch their heads, sweaty from sleep and childhood, I have to force myself to step back and leave them in the hands of the One who created them and gives them each breath. As I turn to leave, I shut the door behind me and let the night come in.

It is dark, yes. Yet the perfume of faithfulness drifts alongside me as I slip into my bed, remembering the sacrifice that a woman not so unlike me made centuries ago. Wafting through my home and all along the roads I travel, the scent of worship is exquisitely, impossibly near. What a glorious choice we have, those of us who have been chosen to carry these losses.

A point came while I was pregnant with Audrey that the Lord showed me that I was going to have to make some hard choices about my walk with Him. I couldn't go on living it out the way I wanted to, the safe way. It was time for me to let down my hair, give it all away, and spend my days spreading word of the glorious riches with which He had blessed me.

But she died, right?

She did.

And to be truthful, I wish it hadn't been this way. As a Christian, I know that I am called to glorify the Lord no matter the circumstance, but that doesn't mean it's going to make sense.

He gives and He takes away. Have I had moments of genuine questioning where I blamed myself and anyone else I could? Yes. But when those thoughts come, and they will, we must make a choice about who we will be from this day forward. Either we will go through life as bitter servants, or we will make Him famous with our love. I want Him to be famous.

The Lord rebuked Judas for his criticism of Mary, saying, "Leave her alone. . . . It was intended that she should save this perfume for the day of my burial" (John 12:7).

I have to admit I had read the story of Lazarus at least a dozen times or more before this last Scripture jumped out at me. I always recognized that Jesus was rebuking Judas, but I hadn't paid attention to the next part. According to Jesus, it was intended that she should use the perfume in exactly the way she had. Does that mean Mary knew Jesus was going to die and be buried shortly? None of the commentaries I found said this; they all agreed that there was no reason to believe she knew why she was doing what she did.

Let's unpack that for a minute because I hope you will be as impacted as I was by what a little more research showed me.

Jesus was aware of His fate as well as Mary's role in the preparation of His body. She, however, was acting out of an urging of the Holy Spirit and felt led to break the bottle and wipe it onto Jesus' feet. Scripture says it was intended that she "should save this perfume." The Greek translation for the word *save* in this passage is *tereo*, a derivative of *teros*, which means "to watch."

Tereo has several meanings, including:

1. To attend carefully
2. To guard
3. To keep
4. To observe
5. To reserve, to undergo something

In other words, the God of the universe had chosen Mary to anoint the body of His precious Son.

He had chosen that night—six days before Passover.

He had chosen that jar—twelve ounces of pure, Indian nard.

He had chosen that woman—Mary, sister of Lazarus and Martha.

And she had no idea.

As I researched this, I had to stop and close my eyes, thinking about the weight of what this meant for me as a servant of Christ. I love visuals, so every time I read a story in the Bible, I want my feet to be dirtied with the same soil they walk, imagining every bit of how that moment felt.

I got up to look through my favorite perfumes and found one that was about the size I pictured hers to be. I turned it upside-down to compare the size, and was shocked to read "1.7 oz."

I thought about the smell that would fill my house if I were to shatter this bottle and the fact that hers was more than six times larger. It was closer to the size of a shampoo bottle than the average perfume bottle.

So she was holding a bottle of perfume, which, according to scholars, would be worth approximately $30,000 in our economy. She shattered it, and as she wiped her hair along Jesus' feet, she had no idea what her role was in bringing God the Father glory. So how can we presume we do?

Every one of us is given alabaster jars in our lives. Moments that have been chosen from before there was time, where we will follow the promptings of the Holy Spirit and glorify our Father with our offering.

Scan back up to the definitions of *tereo* and see if one of them resonates with you. For me I see the picture of reserving or undergoing something one does. Is it possible that we are chosen to undergo something when all the while the Lord knows that it will be given to Him in sweet surrender?

I believe I was.

I believe I am.

I want you to take a few minutes and process the things in your life that are troubling to you; the things you can't seem to understand.

Maybe you have been called to take care of the gift.

Maybe you are guarding it for a day you have yet to see.

Maybe you are watching it, reserving it, waiting for the moment the Lord comes and redeems it all.

And maybe you are just flat-out "undergoing it."

Whatever it is, a loss, a divorce, a death, a hurt, something you feel is out of your control, forgotten by the One who could make it right again—know this.

He has not forgotten.

He heard you call.

He may wait to come to you because He is withholding a blessing in order to give you a better one.

And regardless of whether or not your Lazarus walks out of the tomb, I pray that you continue to worship the Lord, keeping what He has given you until the moment you are called to give it away. And as the glass shatters all around you and you grow dizzy from the intoxicating smell of pure love, get as close to His feet as you can.

And know this.

It was always meant to fall from your hands. And He is glorified in the shattering.

Just as quickly as she had celebrated her brother's resurrection, Mary stood, watching Jesus be crucified. She watched as He was mocked by the crowds of people who hated Him. She saw the wounds He carried when He was lifted into the air by soldiers giddy with the anticipation of His death.

I have to let myself be where she was in order to embrace the depth of sacrifice. I naturally want to distance myself from the horrific truth, but in every thorn in the crown they forced on His head, there is a truth I need to allow to settle on my brow. We serve a God who is aware of our suffering.

As Mary and the others who loved Jesus watched Him, they were overcome with desperation. The Lord Himself cried out in hurt, and they stood helpless, watching as the breath of this life left Him. At some point she left the site of the crucifixion and, I imagine, wandered the streets in sadness to visit and mourn with friends and family.

Here is the part you may not have considered before now. Everywhere she went, every step of the way, *she was followed.* Every person she came into contact with, every stranger who saw her cry, every home she entered was being filled with something intangible, a gift that would be with her for many days to come. It was the scent of love for her Savior, *and it was caught in her hair.*

Close your eyes for a moment and imagine the beauty of this image. She was carrying with her an invisible yet ever-present reminder of who He was to her. Without a single word she told His story over and over again.

I want that.

I want the story of Audrey to be told through the lens of a woman who has smashed the bottle, even in the midst of grief, because I believe that He is Who He says He is.

Be merciful to me, O Lord, for I am in distress;
my eyes grow weak with sorrow,
my soul and my body with grief.
Psalm 31:9

Consider it pure joy, my brothers,
whenever you face trials of many kinds,
because you know that the testing
of your faith develops perseverance.
Perseverance must finish its work so that
you may be mature and complete,
not lacking anything.
James 1:2–4

Chapter 11

Taken

Suddenly, here it is again. The chain of
suggestion can begin almost anywhere: a phrase
heard in a lecture, an unpainted board on a house,
a lamp pole, a stone. From such innocuous things
my imagination winds its sure way to my wound.
Everything is charged with the potential
of reminder. There is no forgetting.
—Nicholas Wolterstorff

While I was pregnant with Audrey, I received a letter from a girl named Sara who was pregnant with a little boy she was planning to name Elliot. She received the same news about her son that I did about Audrey. We spoke at length on the phone and were shocked at the similarities; we actually had the same due date. I felt incredibly blessed to have a sister walking alongside me, albeit hundreds of miles away, whom I could talk to and share what I was going through. We marveled at how the Lord had brought us together and shared the deepest parts of our suffering as the days ticked by and we wondered what the Lord had for our sweet babies.

Sara was scheduled to deliver Elliot three weeks after Audrey, and she also chose a C-section in hopes that she would see him alive. I awoke on April 21 with prayer on my breath and an inexplicable hope for the day. I went to my computer to see if he had been born and there was an e-mail from her aunts saying that not only was he here but he had been born screaming.

Screaming?

But his lungs weren't supposed to be developed.

I wrote the following blog entry as I was processing a hard day, a day that challenged me to continue offering my daughter, as well as myself, to the Lord I trusted.

April 29, 2008

I felt like the Lord was up to something, and I ran out the door with a spring in my step, thinking to myself, What a beautiful day for a miracle.

About an hour later I got a phone call from Todd. He sounded serious. I thought maybe he had heard more about Elliot, but he dropped a bomb I wasn't expecting.

"Angie, I wanted to let you know that Dr. T's office just called. They got the results from Audrey's blood test."

Her diagnosis.

I felt like I couldn't catch my breath. Since early January we had speculated about syndromes and genetic issues. We had wondered what this moment would tell us about her and about why she was, as Ellie called it in prayer, "taken."

"What did it say?" I asked.

"It said nothing, honey. Nothing was wrong. There is no diagnosis. Everything was normal."

I started to cry.

Softly at first and then deeply.

Todd felt terrible.

"I thought it would make you feel better, hon. Why are you crying?"

"I want a reason."

I couldn't see the road through the tears. I am the kind of person that wants to understand exactly what is happening. I can deal with just about anything as long as it can be researched. I pulled into my driveway and called Audra. I sat in the hot car while she listened to the sound of sobbing. She prayed for me, and I wiped my face, trying to get myself together before the kids saw me.

I went straight to the computer to see if Sara's aunts had written.

They had.

Elliot passed away at 9:05 a.m., about an hour after he was born.

I got that far into the e-mail and I slammed my computer shut. I just felt like the wind had whipped through and knocked me down, deep down into a place I didn't want to be.

A place where the answers are fewer than the questions.

A place where God seems hidden, just slightly, by the shadows of this broken life. It is an easy place to get comfortable because all of your hurts are justified and the tears give way to doubt while you meant to pick yourself right back up.

"You could have let him live! Why? What was wrong with my baby? What do You have to gain from all of this loss?"

I literally screamed at the sky while I cried over my own hurt and the hurt of a sister I had never met. He never backs down, though, and I am grateful for that love. It is the love of a Father who Himself is well acquainted with sorrow. It is the love of a Father who has lost His Son. He understands the ranting and the door-slamming. The emptiness that wraps around me when I think of my sweet Audrey.

He knows.

And He only has one request.

Bring it right to Me, Angie.

Every time the anger roars in your heart.

Bring it to Me.

Every time you feel like nobody hears you.

Bring it to Me.

When you think it isn't fair. When you think it isn't true. When you can't think at all.

Bring it to My feet, and I will make an altar from your suffering.

I thought about the day before when Abby had come into the kitchen with a drawing she had made for Audrey. The girls love to draw, and it was a big part of their processing during this time. I looked at it for a few moments and then told her how amazing I thought it was. She had drawn Audrey under a rainbow, standing by a sign that she told me said, "Come see the clowns!"

I'm not sure what the significance of that was, except that Abby did confirm that there are "only clowns in heaven sometimes." That actually made me feel better because I think clowns are kind of creepy.

Abby smiled at me expectantly. I wasn't sure what she was looking for.

"I want to give it to her, Mommy. I want to put it in her basket."

They call her casket a basket, and we don't correct them, because frankly, I like the idea of a basket better anyway.

"OK."

I didn't know what to say. How was I going to explain this to a five-year-old?

She looked at me, waiting.

"So, should we put it in the mailbox, Mommy? Will the man come and get it?"

She wanted to understand the details of our new situation, and the truth at that moment was that I did too.

"Well, Abby, the great thing about heaven is that Audrey can see all of the things that we are doing down here. She can see what you made for her! She can just look right into our house and see it."

I waited to see how this felt to her.

Without a word she spoke life back into my tired bones.

She took the edges of the drawing delicately and lifted it high above her head, closer to her baby sister. She had her head tipped back, looking upward; and after a few seconds she closed her eyes and a smile made its way across her face.

"She liked it, didn't she?" I whispered.

She nodded, still glowing, and ran off to play.

I don't know where you are tonight, or what hurts you are holding up to God, but I will promise you this. If you can just trust Him enough to bring it to Him, He will rejoice in your masterpiece. And if you need to scream a little, know that you have a God who can take that too, as long as your face is tilted (even slightly) toward Him.

Ever-present Counselor, we have to trust You more that we can explain You sometimes.

You are good, Lord.

You are good.

The process of healing has been winding and unpredictable to me. One day I'm starting to feel like myself again, and even that can make me feel guilty sometimes. I feel like I don't have a right to be normal. I used to think that was strange, but after meeting several parents who had gone through the same thing, I realized it was common. A dear woman I know told me that after her teenage son died in a car accident, she was standing at his funeral, and all of a sudden she had the urge to smile. She told me through tear-filled eyes that it was the strangest thing, but that she didn't want to do it because of how crazy everybody would think she was. She told me that as much as it defied what she was feeling, she sensed that it was "the joy of the Lord sneaking up on her."

I loved the way that felt to me. Sometimes I am filled completely with joy, even in the most unlikely situations, and I am learning to accept that for what it is: a gift from the Lord. It hasn't been a linear progression, as much as I would like to say that that was my experience. I have been keenly aware of the way that my grieving looks different from Todd's or even our children's.

As I watch my girls process what has happened, I am constantly seeking the Lord's wisdom in how to parent them through it. Each has her own distinct way of coping, so I try hard to be in touch with the differences. Ellie likes to ask questions about Audrey when we are lying side by side in the dark, and Abby tends to draw pictures and share them with me. Because Kate was a little bit younger, her understanding is less, so mostly she tends to ask what happened to Audrey. I have found that sometimes the Holy Spirit has nudged me to end a conversation for fear of overwhelming them so I try to listen for that urging.

They ask a lot of questions about death and how that will affect them in the future. They want to know if Todd or I am going to die, or whether one of them could, and the truthful answer is yes. I am not just going to leave it there, and as much as I want to go into deep theological exhortations about our eternity with the Lord, I don't. I simply say something like this, "We trust that God has our best at heart, and we will let Him worry about those details. Death isn't something we need to fear because we love Him and we trust Him to take care of us the way He thinks is best."

That usually satisfies them. Sometimes we may get a bit further into a conversation like that, but inevitably it gets to a point where I don't think it's constructive anymore. When that happens, I use one of my favorite parenting techniques, which I read about in *The Hiding Place* by Corrie Ten Boom. Corrie recalls a moment when she asked her father something that was a little too mature for her understanding as far as he was concerned, and he responded with the following:

> He turned to look at me, as he always did when answering a question, but to my surprise he said nothing. At last he stood up, lifting his traveling case from the rack over our heads, and set it on the floor.
>
> "Will you carry it off the train, Corrie?" he said.
>
> I stood up and tugged at it. It was crammed with the watches and spare parts he had purchased that morning.
>
> "It's too heavy," I said.
>
> "Yes," he said. "And I would be a pretty poor father who would ask his daughter to carry such a load. It's the same way, Corrie, with knowledge. Some knowledge is too heavy for children. When you are older and stronger you can bear it. For now you must trust me to carry it for you."
>
> And I was satisfied. More than satisfied—wonderfully at peace. There were answers to this and all my hard questions—for now I was content to leave them in my father's keeping.[1]

What a beautiful example not only for our children but for ourselves as children of the Lord. Many things in this life are not meant to be understood. We are simply not strong enough to bear them, but where there are gaps in our understanding, there is also the grace of God who has chosen to carry the traveling case for us.

Our role is to trust it into His keeping.

---

1. Corrie Ten Boom, *The Hiding Place* (New York, NY: Bantam Books, 1971), 26–27.

Even when I call out or cry for help,
he shuts out my prayer.
He has barred my way with blocks of stone;
he has made my paths crooked.
Lamentations 3:8–9

The LORD is close to the brokenhearted
and saves those who are crushed in spirit.
Psalm 34:18

Chapter 12
Holy Ground

I am standing on the seashore. A ship spreads her
white sails to the morning breeze and starts for the
ocean. I stand watching her until she fades on
the horizon, and someone at my side says, "She is
gone." Gone where? The loss of sight is in me, not in
her. Just at the moment when someone says, "She is
gone," there are others who are watching her com-
ing. Other voices take up the glad shout, "Here she
comes," and that is dying.
—Henry Scott Holland

On the evening of May 27, 2008, I heard my cell phone ring downstairs. It was after ten in the evening, and I wondered who would be calling so late. I was tired so I let it ring.

A moment later my home phone rang, and I started to feel nauseous. Someone doesn't call multiple times this late at night unless something is wrong. I was nervous as I flipped the phone over and saw my mother-in-law's number. I answered quickly, and all I could hear was a deep moaning.

My heart froze.

Immediately I thought of my father-in-law, assuming there had been an accident. Before I could say anything, I heard her groan, "Lukie, *Lukie* . . ."

Luke? What?

"Mom, what's happening? Is he OK?"

"He's not breathing. He's not breathing." She was wailing, barely intelligible. I couldn't get my bearings. I had been half asleep and now I was sitting upright in bed, my heart pounding out of my chest while I fumbled for my glasses.

"What's happening, Mom? We can't lose another one. We can't lose another one, Mom. What's happening over there?" I asked again. I couldn't make any of it make sense.

OK, Ang. Get it together. It isn't going to happen again.

Finally my mother-in-law was able to give us a bit more detail. She said Luke had been asleep for about a half hour and when Nicol went to check on him, he wasn't breathing. They had called 911, and the EMT workers were at their house working on Luke. Greg and Nicol weren't even in the same state as my in-laws, so they were listening as it unfolded, completely helpless.

"So they're trying to revive him?" I asked.

"Yes, they are doing a bunch of things and they . . ." She paused, too overcome with shock to finish.

What I gathered at that moment was that he was having problems breathing and that they were working on him. We invited Todd's sister Shawn, her husband, and their children to come over because they live down the street. It was almost eleven when they pulled into our driveway. Immediately we all huddled together, hysterical with grief.

We tried to talk on the front porch, but we were so distracted. We waited for the phone to ring to tell us he was OK, that we could take the cousins back home in their jammies and praise God that He rescued us from the possibilities. About five minutes after they arrived, the eerie ring filled the house. I looked at the phone, but I couldn't answer it.

Todd's sister was standing next to him, and she covered her face in desperate prayer as he answered the phone.

Todd answered, "Dad? Are you there?"

We couldn't hear her respond so we stared at Todd for any clues. He nodded his head in silence.

"Oh my word, Dad." He looked up at his sister.

"Is he gone? *IS HE GONE*?" she yelled.

Todd nodded slowly, like he was in a daze.

I screamed as loud as I could, and it reached every part of the quiet night around us. I remember spinning around and falling on my doormat, pounding it with my fists over and over, dust rising around me, shouting like an animal out of control. There was no sanity to be grasped, no reality to cling to.

It seemed impossible, but the truth overtook me.

Audrey's cousin Luke was dead seven weeks after her.

I had visions of Nicol, rocking him in her arms at Audrey's burial, and I couldn't seem to wrap my brain around it. He was just here. What happened?

We had the cousins spend the night. We all crawled into our bed in shock, wrapped one another like loops in a quilt. We clung to what we could touch with our hands, because everything else seemed distant, unreal, and unsafe. It was one of the most horrible days of my life, knowing exactly how Nicol would feel when she could process what had happened. When she came face-to-face with the fact that he was gone and he would never come back.

We went to Georgia the next day, and I will never forget the look on Greg's face when I saw him. The only word I can think to use would be *empty*. His eyes were glazed over with grief, and he was slow to move and to speak. We hugged briefly, and out of the corner of my eye I saw Nicol walking toward us. I turned and ran to her, wrapped my arms around her neck, and as her head fell on my shoulder, we let it all go.

We stood there for what seemed like days, clinging to each other, taking turns apologizing for the other's loss. There was a pool in the backyard, and the kids were playing Marco Polo.

It was so surreal.

Just behind me life was moving ahead for the kids while we just sat and stared at each other.

Two moms.

Two babies.

Life in pieces, never to be put back together.

This marked the beginning of a season of questioning for me. While I had felt that way to an extent with Audrey, this was different. I couldn't help but feel like we were being targeted. I knew it wasn't biblical, but in later conversations I discovered that all of us were thinking, *Who's next?* We shielded our kids from activities that might previously have been considered normal play. We were like hawks when they jumped in the pool, every mom secretly waiting for a head to bob up and breathe every time one went under.

I triple-checked my kids' car seats and tiptoed into their room several times at night. Satan whispered to me and tried to convince me that nobody was safe.

The whole family was together for weeks. As we planned the burial and all of the other details, I took on the role of organizer. Not because I was great at it but rather because I had the most experience.

The month after Audrey died, we did it all over again.

We chose a casket.

Another tiny casket.

We made funeral plans and made sure everyone was notified.

But most of all we just sat in our sorrow together. Pictures of Lukie were everywhere. We gathered them around us so that we could just spend time looking at him, imagining who he would have been. Nicol would tell us about how he had just started to move past his colicky stage. Greg would nod his head and mention that he was really starting to see his personality.

We hardly ever got farther than that without just letting the silence and tears come.

I learned during those first days what it had been like for the people who loved us so well a few weeks prior. No wonder they didn't know what to say. No wonder they acted like they were walking on glass. No wonder they felt so incapable, so helpless. And now it was my turn.

Seeing someone you love suffer so desperately with no relief in sight is a dreadful feeling. We tried everything we could, always aware that the break would be momentary, and then we would dig into the hurt again.

My sister-in-law Molly and I were the first ones to go back to the house. It was one of the hardest things I have ever done. I stood in the laundry room looking at a little makeshift changing table. I reached to open the dryer to get some clothes for Greg and Nicol's three-year-old daughter, Summer, when Luke's fresh-smelling clothes came toppling out. I reached for them, pressed them gently to my face, and slipped them back in the dryer, acknowledging that they were sacred and not to be touched for too long.

Out in the front room all of his toys were out; his little swing perched and ready to rock him to sleep. It was waiting in vain. The realization that his little feet wouldn't run in the grass outside was unbearable. A stack of fresh diapers lay right by his playpen, alongside an opened box of wipes. Molly and I worked silently, hardly daring to speak while we sorted through what was left behind.

We gathered what we needed as quickly as possible and left the house, breathing the fresh air outside as deeply as we could. We got in the car, closed the doors behind us, and pulled away—fully aware that we had been standing on holy ground.

We did our best to explain things to our kids, but you don't ever really know what they understand or what is too much for them. My heart was broken for them as I watched them try to put the pieces together. How do you explain something you can't fully understand yourself?

July 9, 2008

> Take off your sandals, for the place
> where you are standing is
> holy ground. (Exodus 3:5)

The funeral home called a few days ago to tell us that Audrey's grave marker was in.

This week has been hard, and for some reason this pushed me over the edge emotionally. I don't even know if I could say it was sadness because I have been waiting for weeks for this call. I wanted her to have more than the little plastic placeholder with the piece of paper in it. I was relieved that it was finally there, but it took my breath away to hear the words. It feels so final.

Immediately I told Todd I wanted to go over and see it. We only have one car right now (I kind of wrecked the other one a little bit, but I contend that it was the pile of cement's fault. It practically jumped out and ripped off my bumper), and the twins had a friend over, so I started out the door. Kate saw me grab my keys, and she started screaming and begging to come with me. I told her that I was going to see Audrey and then to the grocery store and that I didn't think she would have as much fun as if she stayed and played with all the girls. She protested. And then she started putting on her shoes and saying over and over, "Ona go, Momma. Ona go." When Kate says she "wants to" go, she is pretty persistent. I didn't have the strength to fight her, so I told her she could come. She ran to the playroom and grabbed the back page of a princess magazine they had been reading, wiped her eyes, and said, "Let's go, Momma. I go wif you, just you and Kate, Momma. Just us, right?"

"Just you and me, Kate. We're going to go see Audrey." She climbed in her car seat, clinging to the magazine page.

The whole way to the cemetery, I watched her smile in the rearview mirror. I love taking each of my girls out for alone time because we get to connect in a different way than when we are all together, and I think it helps them to know they are each so special to me. Kate really needs this time, especially lately.

We got to the cemetery, and I grabbed my camera to take pictures so Todd could see Audrey's marker. I obliged when Kate asked to take off her shoes. She loves the feeling of grass in her toes; she is the kind of kid who wants to feel everything fully. She wants to touch the flowers (pluck mercilessly), to sort my purse (turn upside down and use up my new lipstick), and to enjoy her food (shove fistfuls into her mouth while closing her eyes and purring "mmm-mmm"). She doesn't know how to do life halfway, and I love that about her.

She grabbed her little page and started walking around the cemetery with this big grin. I spent some time talking to Audrey and then asked Kate if she wanted to come over with me (she had discovered the joy of stealing the little flags from several vases . . . don't worry, they have been returned).

She looked up at me, confused.

"Ona see Audrey."

"She's right here, honey. They just gave her a special new plaque that tells about her. It has her name on it." I ran my fingers along the letters, and she took a step in my direction, then stopped.

"Ona see her, Momma. Where is she? Where is Audrey?"

Tears filled my eyes as I realized what was happening. She thought that we were going to see Audrey. The Audrey she held, not the one who is under this marker. The Audrey that wore a dress and looked like a baby doll. That's why she had been smiling the whole way here. No wonder she wanted to come with me so badly. She probably wondered why it had taken us so long to go back to see her. I didn't know what to say. She kept looking at me, clutching her little page.

"What did you bring, Kate?" I studied her face.

"A book for Audrey. I give it to her." She looked at the grave and then looked at me.

"OK, honey. Let's give it to Audrey." I couldn't see through the tears because in that moment my emotions did not stretch farther than the bounds of her two-and-a-half year-old brain. I couldn't stand it either. We should be reading books at home with her, not sobbing together in the middle of a cemetery.

Oh Lord Jesus, come be near to us. Hold us with Your unfailing love. We cannot sustain ourselves.

She bent down and gingerly set the page on her sister's grave.

I read the words over and over in those moments:

Audrey Caroline Smith
April 7, 2008

Not many words.

Not many hours.

So many tears.

I cannot seem to find my way these past few days. I have bruises on my legs from bumping into furniture that has not moved in years. I got lost driving home the other night from a familiar place and didn't even realize I was lost until I had been driving in the wrong direction for almost fifteen minutes. All day long I forget the most simple words, the most familiar faces, the words to a song I know by heart. Sometimes I just stand in the shower with the water scalding my skin so that I can feel something that registers. My brain just doesn't know its way around the sorrow.

I know all of these things are part of the process, or so my grief books say. I have stacks of them piled up by my bed, nestled on shelves, stored on the coffee tables. They are to be my road map through this valley, and yet in this moment all of the words are just meaningless. I know this is normal, but I assure you, it is anything but.

We figured out a way to tuck Kate's gift into the back of Audrey's vase so that it wouldn't blow away. Kate cried as we walked back to the car because she finally realized we were not going to "see" Audrey. I put her sandals back on her dirty feet and wiped her cheeks clean. Then I wiped mine clean as well.

As I drove away, I looked back at the roses, and I couldn't help but process the fact that she would never walk down a long aisle with a bouquet of fresh flowers.

Oh, Audrey, how we miss you.

"Why does your face look so sad when you are not ill?
This can be nothing but sadness of heart."
Nehemiah 2:2

Do not be anxious about anything,
but in everything, by prayer and petition,
with thanksgiving, present your requests to God.
And the peace of God, which transcends all understanding,
will guard your hearts and your minds in Christ Jesus.
Philippians 4:6–7

Chapter 13
Since She Left

*Grief is like a long valley, a winding valley where
any bend may reveal a totally new landscape. As
I've already noted, not every bend does. Sometimes
the surprise is the opposite one; you are presented
with exactly the same sort of country you thought
you had left behind miles ago. That is when you
wonder whether the valley isn't a circular trench.
But it isn't. There are partial recurrences, but the
sequence doesn't repeat.* —C. S. Lewis

So what is it like to live life after losing a child?

I guess that depends on the day.

So many people have written to me and asked how the grieving process has been for me, and to be honest, I never know how
to answer. I have a master's degree in psychology and I know the
steps of grief. They look great on paper along with all the other mul-
tiple-choice questions, but in reality they aren't that simple. They
jump back and forth at a pace that is completely unpredictable.

A perfect example of this happened a few days ago. I was doing really well and felt like I had turned a corner in some sense. I was out with the girls running some errands, when out of the corner of my eye I saw a little redheaded girl toddling near me, and I looked up at her mother.

"She just started this. She's trying to get her balance." She laughed and chased after her.

I watched them until they disappeared from view.

And the next thing I knew, I was grabbing onto the rack next to me, trying to catch my breath. I have those moments constantly where I imagine who she would have been, and I have to grieve each stage differently. I've been told it's normal.

But it's really different when it's happening. You catch yourself doing things that a sane person wouldn't do, and yet it doesn't seem like there's another logical option. It's really a delicate balance between letting yourself grieve the way you need to and functioning in a world that keeps reminding you of what you have lost.

In the months that followed Audrey's death, I would find myself absentmindedly walking up and down the baby aisle, smelling shampoo and looking at tiny diapers. If you have never lost a baby, this probably sounds strange, but to me it was part of the process. The truth is that to some degree, every day I have here is another day without her. I don't know when I will be able to see life any differently.

If you are walking through this yourself or with someone you love, know that every day is going to feel different. There is no systematic way to understand the process, and I know because I have highlighted it all in books and then tossed them in the trash.

I don't know what tomorrow is going to look like. Quite frankly, I don't know what an hour from now is going to look like.

And that's fine.

It's not a twelve-step program.

It's life after loss, and it's not going anywhere. I have to learn to go easier on myself and back down off my expectations because I am setting myself up for failure. I can't tell you how many times I told myself that a truly strong Christian woman would have done this or that differently. I get so irritated at myself, thinking, *well, she didn't have this issue.* Or *maybe if I trusted the Lord more, I wouldn't hurt this badly.*

I finally started expressing these thoughts to women around me who had lost children. I was absolutely shocked to hear that I wasn't alone. We all grieve differently, and we all hide portions of it in places we wouldn't dare let others see. I have been reminded that I am daily battling an enemy who would love nothing more than for me to shove all my baggage into the crevices of darkness, slam the doors, and pretend I have it all together while I secretly fall apart. As I lie in bed at night and wonder what I could have done differently, he laughs victoriously. He looks on while my marriage suffers and I play the role of happy homemaker because everyone else seems to have their act together.

Hear me say this, please.

I have believed him more times than I can say.

I have imagined myself to be the only one, and ironically women were looking to me to be a role model for grief. So I had to be honest with myself and with them. I want to be honest with you because I don't want you to let the devil steal from you what does not belong to him. Tell him he cannot have this life from you, nor can he have your thoughts, your family, or your faith.

Will you allow me to take a moment and pray for you?

Lord Jesus, I am asking for Your presence to fill the room of the person holding this book. I ask that You remind him or her that Your power is made perfect in weakness and that the battle raging against us is no match for You. In Your powerful name, I command Satan to leave this home.

Leave this marriage alone. Stop whispering lies about the circumstances of death and the belief that we could have done anything differently. Silence the lies the enemy has thrown to us. You have no right here, Satan, and we rebuke you in the name of the Savior. Jesus, bind his hands so that he will no longer wreak havoc in the lives of these precious parents. Lord, we give You our hurts, our doubts, our guilt. We bring them to you and lay them on Your altar, eagerly awaiting the day when You will redeem what we have lost. Amen.

One of the things I did as I walked through this dark time was to journal what I was feeling. As I look back on those words, I feel that God heals me in ways I didn't anticipate. I can see the way my heart has softened and remember details about Audrey I may not have. If you're going through a similar situation, I encourage you to document as much as possible whether it be through journaling, photography, video, art, or whatever medium works for you.

Set aside time to be still with the Lord. In the hustle and bustle of life, you will be urged to move more quickly than you should. Having time set aside for this purpose will help you maintain focus. I suggest choosing a topic (grace, mercy, loss, redemption, gratitude, sadness) and begin to study what the Bible says about it. A good concordance is really helpful for this. I love to light a candle, find a familiar, comfortable spot, and focus on seeking His face. I have a little area set up with plenty of pens, notebooks, and favorite books to fill my mind with images of truth. I may have only a few minutes, but I always find that I am more settled when I slide my chair back under the table, processing the fact that no matter where I am, He meets me there.

None of us grieves the same way, and one of the best things we can do is to give ourselves permission to live that out. For me that has meant facing things in myself that I have always known were problematic (I am a people pleaser through and through) and changing the way I allowed them to run my life. Sometimes it takes something drastic happening for you to shift a boundary line, and for me losing Audrey did that.

For example, I have found that there are some people in my life I don't feel as comfortable being myself around. It isn't because they aren't great people but more because I feel an obligation to befriend them in a way I'm not capable of anymore. They need more of me than I can give, and I have gotten better about not spreading myself so thin. Instead of booking every minute solid so that I could make sure everything was taken care of for everyone else, I have made a point to have time just to sit in my sorrow. That sounds strange to say, but whenever I am in a hard place emotionally, my first instinct is to fill up my calendar and make sure I have another person beside me at all times. There are certainly times when being in community is necessary and beneficial, but for me it became a way to run from being alone with the Lord, and I began to suffer because of it. He wanted me to be still and to let Him take care of me instead of depending on everyone else to do it. I won't say I'm great at it yet, but I'm better.

I also had to start saying the sentence I have avoided for most of my life: "I need you to do this." It's always been easy to extend myself beyond what was humanly possible and then beat myself up when I failed. I am trying to do less of this, and when I started to back down from commitments and expectations, some people didn't know how to handle it. If you have walked through something similar, I am sure you have images of a person or group of people that meet this description, and I am praying for you as you discern who is a blessing and who is a burden. You may need to reprioritize your relationships in order to grieve in an authentic way. This can be a challenge, but it is worth it. I have found that I am delaying the inevitable if I continue to surround myself with people who are pushing me toward normalcy before I am ready.

A lot of women in the midst of loss ask me how long it will be until they get better, and my honest answer is that I don't feel much better yet. I feel different, and I may have more gaps between really bad days, but the pain isn't going away. And you know what? That's OK.

Part of my purpose in this life is to be Audrey's voice, and I do this with great pride and a tremendous amount of prayer. I wish she had lived. I would be lying if I said I am always completely at peace with how things turned out.

I am also learning to separate *what I feel* from *the One I serve*, and the distinction is where the beauty of life is able to return.

In his amazing work on loss, *Turn My Mourning into Dancing*, Henri Nouwen says something that has shaped many of my decisions since Audrey has been gone.

> Our choice, then, often revolves around not what has
> happened or will happen to us, but how we will relate
> to life's turns and circumstances. Put another way: Will
> I relate to my life resentfully or gratefully?[1]

I could have easily slipped into a life of resentment after we lost Audrey, sometimes even now I consciously have to fight that tendency. Maybe you are walking through a situation right now that makes you feel abandoned by the Lord. When people come to me and ask how I have such a genuine, trusting love for Christ, it really comes down to the daily decision I have to make to live my life gratefully.

Part of trying to cultivate a grateful heart is looking for opportunities to share the gospel through my loss and seeking ways to bring God glory through the loss. When I feel like hiding in my room and ignoring the world, I start to feel depressed, and the resentment sinks in. Picking yourself up and going about your life as if it's all a gift isn't easy when you have lost something so precious.

But that's just it; I can either focus on what I have lost, or what I have gained, and I choose the latter.

Sometimes I have to choose it a couple of times an hour.

Henri Nouwen speaks to this need:

> And so we wait patiently, if the situation requires it, watching for gifts to come where we are. Look at the wonderful, exuberant flowers painted by the famous Dutch artist Vincent van Gogh. What grief, what sadness, what melancholy he experienced in his difficult life! Yet what beauty, what ecstasy! Looking at his vibrant paintings of sunflowers, who can say where the mourning ends and the dance begins? *Our glory is hidden in our pain, if we allow God to bring the gift of himself in our experience of it.* If we turn to God, not rebelling against our hurt, we let God transform it with greater good. We let others join in and discover it with us.[2]

And herein lies the dance we will do for the rest of our lives.

It is a dance that was begun before we were born, long before the music even began to play. What the Lord has given us can either be taken into ourselves as pain or given back to Him as a holy offering, one that glorifies His name and gives meaning to our loss.

> If mourning and dancing are part of the same movement of grace, we can be grateful for every moment we have lived. We can claim our unique journey as God's way to mold our hearts to greater conformity to Christ. The cross, the primary symbol of our faith, invites us to see grace where there is pain; to see resurrection where there is death. The call to be grateful is a call to trust that

every moment can be claimed as the way of the cross that leads to new life.[3]

About a year after we lost Audrey, I was invited to be a part of an amazing experience. I traveled to India with several other bloggers on a trip with the organization, Compassion International. I am absolutely petrified of flying, and I would never have considered it if it hadn't been for Audrey. In so many ways she has made me brave. She made me want to be a better mommy, a better wife, a better daughter to the King who holds her in His arms.

We went to the slums of Calcutta, and I had the opportunity to go to Mother Teresa's orphanage. I will never forget a conversation I had with one of the workers there when I asked about a tiny baby in the front of the room. She looked to be no more than two or three weeks old. I asked the woman her name. In broken English she told me that they didn't bother to give them names because the Father would probably be calling them home soon.

When she walked away, I lingered with the infant, and I ran my fingers up and down her little legs and sang to her. She turned her head toward me when she heard the sound, and I looked into her eyes. Eventually it was time to leave, and I cried as I walked away, knowing that in that moment the Lord had confirmed something I felt strongly but hadn't vocalized. I want to be a voice for my daughter, and I want to use what I have walked through to bring other people to Him. Too much is happening in the world for us to sit back and ignore what we are being called to, and for me that stems from my love of children.

Before I went to India, I asked Compassion International to choose a little girl for my family to sponsor, and if possible, I wanted to have a child who shared Audrey's birthday of April 7. It turned out that there was only one child in India that matched that criteria in their system, and she didn't live anywhere near where we were going to be. Everyone was going to meet their sponsor children except for me because they weren't sure how they could get her to Calcutta.

At least that's what they told me.

It turns out that they had made arrangements in advance for her, her father, and one of her schoolteachers to take a train ride to where we were. It was the first time any of them had ever left their tiny village, and they spent twenty-four hours on a train.

It took longer for her to get to me than it did for me to get to India.

I walked into the hotel lobby where she was waiting for me, and there are no words that could describe what I felt when I saw her. She was a beautiful seven-year-old with huge brown eyes and a fleeting, hesitant smile. I reached out my hand to her, and then without any thought I took her into my arms as our translator explained what I was saying. I told her about Audrey, and she nodded sadly. Then I told her that she and Audrey had the same birthday and that she was special to me because of her connection to my daughter. I told her that Todd and I were going to write to her and that we would be praying for her all the time. We spent the day hand in hand, a connection that words fail to capture. In those hours I talked to her about how much the Lord loved her and the great purposes He had for her life. I showed her how to use a fork and laughed with her as her food flew across the table.

Before she got back on the bus to begin her long journey home, I gave her a special doll that was made to look just like her. A Scripture I selected for her was written on her stomach. I smoothed the doll's dress over her little belly and handed her to this precious child who was waiting to touch her new doll.

The translator stood close by, and I asked him to tell her a few more things. As my sweet new friend played with the doll's hair,

I said, "Tell her that the Lord knows how many hairs are on her head and He loves her in a way she cannot even begin to imagine."

I started to cry as he translated and her eyes grew wide.

She hugged the doll and whispered something in return. I looked to the translator.

"She says she is proud to know you, and she would like for you to send her a picture of your family. She would like to see your children."

As he finished, she said another short sentence.

"What did she say?" I asked.

"She said, 'All of them.' Do you know what this means?"

"Yes." I was choking on my own sadness, and I reached to her. A little girl who shared only a birthday with my Audrey, and she was already so dear to me. I whispered, "Thank you" in her ear and she squeezed me tightly.

Nobody needed to translate that.

A few minutes later it was time for her to board her bus, and all of us stood outside as our new "children" walked away from us. We knew that realistically we probably wouldn't see them again, and they knew it as well. Not a dry eye could be found and we all leaned out as far as we could as the bus pulled away.

In my mind's eye I will forever carry that image, because it reminded me of that same month a year prior.

I only had a short time with her, but that didn't make the good-bye any easier. Even if I never see her again on this side of eternity, one thing is sure.

She knows she is loved by the One who never lets go.

A new chapter had begun for me.

And it will for you as well.

---

1. Henri Nouwen, *Turn My Mourning into Dancing: Finding Hope in Hard Times* (Nashville, TN: Thomas Nelson, 2001), 12.
2. Ibid., 15, emphasis added.
3. Ibid., 18.

I tell you the truth, you will weep and mourn
while the world rejoices.
You will grieve,
but your grief will turn to joy.
(John 16:20)

My eyes will flow unceasingly, without relief,
until the LORD looks down
from heaven and sees.
Lamentations 3:49–50

The LORD your God is with you,
he is mighty to save.
He will take great delight in you,
he will quiet you with his love,
he will rejoice over you with singing.
Zephaniah 3:17

Chapter 14
Burden Carriers

Sorrow is one of the things that are lent, not given.
A thing that is lent may be taken away;
a thing that is given is not taken away.
Joy is given;
sorrow is lent.
We are not our own,
we are bought with a price . . .
[Our sorrow] is lent us for just a little while
that we may use it for eternal purposes.
Then it will be taken away
and everlasting joy will be
our Father's gift to us,
and the Lord God will wipe away
all the tears from off all faces.
—Amy Carmichael

Many people have asked me how they can help friends who are in a similar situation. Similarly, many have asked what they should avoid doing. I know that everyone deals with grief differently, but one of the things that meant the world to me was that people acknowledged that we had lost her. It is really awkward to be walking around and see someone who knows what happened but doesn't say anything. I always knew people were doing this to protect me, and their motives were pure, but it was so much easier when they would just ask about it. When it didn't come up, I felt like she wasn't real. I wanted her to be acknowledged. Regardless of whether the loss is an early term miscarriage or the loss of a child, this was a life that had been entrusted to me as a parent, and I wanted her to be recognized.

Several days after Audrey died, I ran into someone I hadn't seen in a while, but she knew what I had been through. She told me how sorry she was and reached out to hug me. I rested my chin on her shoulder for a moment, and when we stepped out of the embrace, she looked at me with a loving smile.

"Tell me about her, Angie. Everything."

She wanted to know about her hair, her eyes, if she made noises—everything.

She wanted to know my girl.

It meant the world to me, and many other moms who have walked through something similar have told me the same.

I feel blessed to be in a generation where these conversations take place because most of the women I have spoken to in my parents' generation had a much different experience. They have sketched for me an image of what it was like to lose a child back then, and it feels inhumane. When Todd tells the story of Audrey at concerts, the Holy Spirit sometimes prompts him to ask women who have lost a child to stand.

It is unusual for less than half to stand.

I cannot begin to count the women who have come up to me or to Todd after the concert and say that this was the first time their babies were ever acknowledged.

One woman came to me in tears, and I could tell she hadn't shared her burdens often. She was searching for words, reaching into the air for descriptions she hadn't looked for before. I asked her to walk with me, and we found a quiet spot on a couch just out of the way of the crowd. She told me about the time, more than thirty years ago, when she was pregnant with her first son. The pregnancy had been uneventful, and she went into labor with eager anticipation. Much of the delivery was a blur to her, but she remembered them telling her that her son was sick and that they were going to take him into another room to assess him more closely.

A few minutes later the doctor came back into the room and told her that her son was dead and that there was nothing they could do. She asked him if she could hold him, and the doctor told her it wasn't a good idea because she wouldn't want to let him go. He told her it was best just to go on without meeting him. Her husband, who hadn't been present for the delivery, was saddened but agreed that it was best just to move on.

Her eyes glazed over as she explained that when she was released from the hospital, she and her husband walked to the car without a word about what had happened.

And to that day they still hadn't talked about their loss.

I cried with her, feeling her hurt as if it were my own, imagining what it would have been like for me to be in that situation.

She continued, explaining, "I thought that was the worst of it, but it wasn't." I couldn't imagine what was coming next.

She had a crumpled Kleenex between her hands, and she held it to her mouth, about to say something to a stranger that she had never shared before with anyone.

"I got his death certificate in the mail several weeks later, and it had his official time of death. Angie, he didn't die that morning. He died almost nine hours later."

I gasped in disbelief.

"I know they were trying to protect me. I know that. But my son was with strangers. I could have been holding him, and he never knew . . . he never knew . . ."

Her head collapsed into her hands, and I reached out to hold her.

"He knew," I whispered. "He knew you."

She shook with an unexplored grief when I said those words because for years she had been walking around with hurt she didn't think mattered. Her mother-in-law had told her she just needed to forget the whole thing and toughen up. She said she had been trying—and failing—to do so for more than thirty years.

She went on to say that she had two other children who were grown, neither aware of the boy who had been their brother.

Thirty years.

I have been stunned speechless at the number of women who have come to me with similar stories. One of the common veins is the feeling that they had to "move on," "get over it," "appreciate what they have," and similar suggestions. I can tell you as a mother who has experienced losing a baby: it isn't going to happen. Grief is a winding, nasty road that has no predictable course, and the best thing you can do as a friend is to show up for the ride. *You cannot rush grief.* Read that again, and let it soak in as you either walk through it or alongside someone who is in the midst of it.

One of the best things you can do for friends who are suffering through loss is to remind them of this over and over. Don't mention how other people have "coped so well" with their losses or how "it seems like so-and-so has come out of this better than you have." I have heard from people who have heard these exact sentences, and while I have a feeling their friends wanted to encourage them into a place of recovery, they weren't helped by such remarks. It stings to feel like your grief isn't normal or that you aren't recovering the way you should be.

There is no normal. There is the loss, and there is the Lord. That balance dictates the season, not the changing leaves or the anniversaries of death.

I love the way Gregory Floyd explains the delicate balance of hope and pain, "Our faith gives us the sure hope of seeing him again, but the hope does not take away the pain."[1]

People are uncomfortable swimming in another's grief. The way they respond to it is, naturally, to try and fix the situation. Of course, they can't, but letting just the silence hang there feels wrong, so they try to fill it with words they think will help. I sense people's intentions, and I know that this is their desire, but honestly it falls flat. It means so much more to me when people just tell me they're sorry and don't try to make all the pieces fit or explain it into something that it isn't. I know how it feels to be on the other side as well, and I understand that you want to say the right thing. Yet sometimes the right thing is to say nothing at all. It's just to be there, available, willing, authentic.

Nicol told me of a time shortly after Luke passed away that a woman who was a prayer warrior came to her and embraced her, sobbing as if she herself was carrying Nicol's burden. No pretty words were said, only the arms of a woman who made herself present and invited herself into the sorrow. It's a place most people run from, and it's refreshing and healing when people enter in. People's natural instincts are to rush us through our grieving because they love us so much. A time will come when we are ready to take the next step, but that is between the Lord and ourselves. In the meantime, please be sensitive to those who are grieving, aware that they may not be able to do "normal" things for a while.

In addition, know that some things are going to be hard, not because anyone wants to be hurtful, but simply because they exist. It's hard to walk past a baby nursery or see someone's baby announcement in the front yard. If you are close to a person who has lost a child, try to be sensitive to his or her feelings. I truly wanted to celebrate other people's newborns, but it was hard to do. I believe how difficult the situation is often comes down to the way the other person approaches it. Several people made simple statements such as, "Is it really hard for you to be around the baby?" or, "I can't imagine what you're feeling now. I just want to acknowledge that I care about you and that I haven't forgotten that you're still walking a long road." These simple statements of consideration meant the world to me and blessed me by allowing me to celebrate more authentically with them.

Sometimes it was just too much to talk at all. I have a small circle of friends with whom I can just be silent. They would take me right where I was and were so wonderful about shifting their words to meet me there. There were moments that I needed to laugh and pretend to be normal because I couldn't physically bear the hurt. Other times (maybe even five minutes later), I would break down and question everything from God to why there was a stain on my carpet. I felt crazy sometimes, like nothing I was saying made sense. To have friends who sat beside me while I dealt with everything was wonderful.

On a practical level I was still a mother to three children, and keeping up with all of my regular mom duties was hard. People brought us meals for months, and it was an enormous blessing to have one less thing to worry about every day.

I'm sure many of you can relate to the fact that it isn't easy to accept help. At first I really struggled with this, thinking about other people who surely deserved it more. After all, I could physically make our dinner, right? A dear friend sat me down and told me that not only did I need help, but I was also taking an opportunity away from those who wanted to minister to me by refusing it.

Looking back, I realize how many opportunities this provided me just to be present with family, which was our greatest need.

It may seem like a small thing to bring over a casserole in light of what has happened, but believe me when I say you have no idea how much it will be appreciated. I have talked to many other mothers who say the same. They tell me that after losing their children, they couldn't seem to get normal things done, and to have meals available made a huge difference.

We had friends come over and play with the girls, do laundry, sweep the floors, mow the lawn, and drop off thoughtful gifts. I felt more gratitude than I knew how to express because grief made me not want to do anything other than survive. I don't know how I would have gotten through those days without the generosity of friends who carried me.

I am also one of those people who never want to let anyone down or feel like I am a burden, so I struggled with feeling like I needed to jump back into certain activities or relationships before I was really ready. Doing even the minimum was so hard on most days that the rest of what I needed to do fell by the wayside. It took me a long time before I was able to put appropriate boundaries up without feeling guilty.

On a practical level I am so glad that I was referred to Now I Lay Me Down to Sleep, an organization that exists in most cities and specializes in photographing infants that are expected to pass away after birth or in the womb after twenty-five weeks. Some days it feels like that's all we have left of our precious Audrey, and it makes her memory come to life. I am so grateful to have these amazing photographs to share with my daughters when they are older. Even now they ask to take them out and look at them. Seeing the photographs helps them process what they are feeling because the pictures are so much more tangible than the grief itself.

Many people have asked what we did to memorialize Audrey. I have been inspired by the stories I've received from others in response to the same question. We really wanted to do things that helped others. Because of our involvement with a local organization, we were able to do that. We are proud supporters of The Hope Clinic in Nashville, which counsels pregnant women who are considering abortion. Several months after Audrey was born, they opened a home designed to house a few mothers who had chosen life for their babies. One of the bedrooms is called "Audrey's Room." The offerings we received from generous friends, family, and blog readers went to this valuable cause, and it meant so much to me to walk into that bright place, a celebration of life, and know that she was a part of it.

This is a personal preference although I have met other moms who felt the same after they lost their children. The things people did for us or gave us were the most meaningful when they had more than a temporal significance. I love flowers, but every bouquet I received was one I was going to have to watch die. This saddened me, reminding me of how temporal her life was. When I see her name on a plaque, or on a necklace, on a memorial foundation, or anything similar, it bears more weight for me. She was a real person, and I want her to be remembered. As you help a friend who is grieving loss, try to find ways to memorialize the child in a way that has a lasting impact. Maybe there's an organization you could donate to on the child's behalf, a tree you could plant in the baby's honor, or a song you can write. You could make something for the family that incorporates the child's name and can be enjoyed for years to come. I received a Bible with Audrey's name printed on it and cried when I opened it because it was so personal. I also love the idea of taking the baby's clothing and piecing it together in a quilt or making a shadowbox with mementos that were important, such as a baby rattle, favorite toy, dress, footprints, or other items.

The most important thing you can do to help someone who is in the depths of loss is to pray. Make notes on your calendar to write periodically, call out of nowhere, and read a psalm to your friend that you think will minister to her. The more you pray for her, the more in tune you will be with how the Holy Spirit is desiring to use you in her life, and that makes all the difference. Sometimes I meet people that I know I am probably never going to see again, and I make a point of asking for wisdom, even as we are shaking hands and exchanging names. I ask the Lord to reveal to me what He is calling me to speak into that person's life. As long as I am faithful to His leading, I know something will penetrate. Be on your knees for your friends and commit to seeing it through, however long that takes. Believe that the Lord can use you, because He can.

Essentially what I am encouraging you to do as a burden carrier is twofold. Show up ready to walk alongside the one who grieves and commit to lifting that person up to the Lord in prayer. I assure you, you cannot mess up a conversation with someone who is going through this season as long as you are doing these things. The Holy Spirit will quiet you and allow you to be available in a way that will minister to your friend for years to come.

> *Lord, enable these sweet readers to feel equipped through Your Holy Spirit. Let them be vessels of your goodness and messengers of hope to those who have none. Whisper to them as they rest, reminding them to pray. When they wake in the morning, bring to mind those who grieve. We trust that Your Word will not return void, and we offer all of these prayers to You. We beseech You to turn them into more; make them small enough to fit into the deepest, darkest crevices of hurt and enable us to be sacrificial enough to dig farther. Let us be the body of Christ to those who need us in a way that brings glory to You, Jesus. Amen.*

I cannot finish this chapter without mentioning a question I receive often and feel strongly about answering.

"Where is my baby now?"

I will share with you my firm belief on the matter, hoping it brings you some degree of comfort.

I believe that *all* babies who pass away (including those who did not survive outside the womb) are in heaven with our Lord. I do not believe they vanish into the ground, or that they ever endure any suffering or pain when they leave us. I cling to the fact that Audrey is in her eternal home, enjoying the favor of her Savior, completely at peace with Him as her Father.

I believe it, but I can't honestly say that it always comforts me the way I wish it would. I say that because I know that some of you who are reading are in the same place I am. I know you long to drop a weight off your back and carry on with life in complete joy, never doubting that everything will be set right one day. It's not easy, and I would be lying if I said that when I sit in my sewing room staring at the bloodstains on the collar of her little dress, I am immediately filled with peace because I know where she is. I am not. I want her to be here with me, and on many nights that truth has failed to fill the void. I have beaten myself up many times, wondering why I was moping around when she was perfectly happy. What kind of Christian does that?

The answer is pretty simple actually.

One who is human.

We aren't going to feel whole in this life, and we will long for something we don't have. Something that will fill the nagging void that intermittently stings and knocks us to our knees. And all the while, Satan taunts us, telling us our faith is small. To hurt so deeply is a sign that we live in a fallen world, not that we serve a small God.

To love Him in spite of our pain is a gift He freely gives to those who will accept it.

Daily I must remind myself that He is not threatened by my doubt nearly as much as He is glorified by my faith. We are vessels of hope, you and I, made in the image of Jesus, breathing in this world as we yearn for Him.

Is it hard to believe that my baby is in heaven? Yes. I can't see it, so I am trusting that my faith is real. I do believe it, but no, I don't think it's easy when you have empty arms and your baby is in an unreachable place. That's why they call it faith, I guess.

I have asked the Lord to show me signs of her, to encourage me to believe she is with Him, and He has been faithful many times in honoring that request.

I was talking to Greg on the phone a few weeks after Luke died. He was on his way home from playing golf. He choked up while telling me that as he played he realized he would never have the chance to play golf with Luke, and he was forced to let go of another small dream he had had as a father. I totally understood because oftentimes I will be in the middle of some mundane task or experience and just ache to be able to share it with Audrey.

I was silent on the other end as I listened, and finally I started crying too. At the time Abby and Ellie were upstairs watching a movie, and Kate was taking a nap.

Later that day they were drawing together while I fixed supper, and Abby came in with a picture she had drawn. I asked her what it was, and she told me it was a picture of Luke and Audrey in heaven together. I couldn't really make out anything but their faces, so I asked her to tell me about it.

"They're happy, Mommy. And they're playing together."

I asked her if they were playing at the park. She shook her head no and pointed to something I hadn't seen.

"No," she said confidently. "They're playing golf."

Even now I find myself at a loss for words when thanking those who gathered around me and helped me through such a painful time. I am sitting cross-legged in an overstuffed chair, coffee steaming beside me as I realize I am now writing from the other side of the hardest days of my trial. It is a day I never imagined I would have to face, and it has made me aware of my own mortality. We are not guaranteed anything in this life, and without the hope of Jesus, I would have been swept away with the tides the last years have brought.

In Him and only Him, I stand firm.

Toes in the water, staring out into the great landscape He has painted for me, I bravely step out farther every day. I know that as soon as I reach the place where my feet no longer touch the ocean floor, He will carry me into the distance, all the while reminding me He has never left me.

I hope that you believe these words, and that your soul is resting in the joy He brings in the midst of the storm.

Now walk, love.

He is waiting.

And so are they.

> ***This is why I weep***
> ***and my eyes overflow with tears.***
> ***No one is near to comfort me,***
> ***no one to restore my spirit.***
> ***Lamentations 1:16***

> ***He heals the brokenhearted***
> ***and binds up their wounds.***
> ***Psalm 147:3***

1. Gregory Floyd, *A Grief Unveiled: One Father's Journey through the Death of a Child* (Brewster, MA: Paraclete Press, 1999), 85.

Chapter 15
A Letter to My Daughter

Death lies on her, like an untimely frost upon the sweetest flower of all the field.
—William Shakespeare

Sweet Audrey,

There are no words I could say in this letter that could express what you are to us, but I feel compelled to write them anyway.

Do you know you changed the world?

From the day we found out we were expecting you, we knew that God had chosen you for our family. When we started feeling you move around, we invented stories about who you would be. We took bets on whether you were a boy or a girl (Daddy was wrong!). Abby and Ellie set aside toys they wanted to give to you. Your daddy let me buy books at the bookstore about being pregnant, even though we already have a million. He knows I love the smell of books, and he just watched with a smile while I gathered them together. We talked about you all the time. Our house was filled with love for you long before we ever knew who you would be to us. We let Kate help us set up a crib in her room while we told her that she was going to have a baby brother or sister sleeping next to her someday. We introduced her little toddler bed and taught her all about being a big sister. She loved her freedom. We found her in the pantry eating chocolate at 3:00 a.m. one night! And so for weeks, we planned. We talked about names, about paint, about schools, about everything but the one thing we didn't know.

God had something much bigger planned for your life than we could ever have imagined.

On January 7, we heard the beginning of the story. You kicked while I listened to them tell me that I should let you go. You, unable to say a word, spoke volumes as we considered what had been laid before us. Audrey, we never had a choice. You were ours from the moment God ordained it so. There were moments in the darkness during that time when I worried that maybe we should give you to God. We didn't want you to suffer, and we knew that as soon as you were with Him, you would be at peace. Were we self-ish for trying to keep you here? We knew before we let ourselves travel into those thoughts that they were lies. That decision was not for us to make. We settled into the reality of "our new life," and the stacks of books on pregnancy gave way to Scripture.

Did you know that while you were in my tummy, you went to the beach, to Disney World, to the ballet, to the zoo, to the sym-phony, to pick out our puppy, to the children's theater, to listen to Daddy sing, to church, to Poppy's house . . . and so many more places? I talked to you about how the laundry machine worked, told you about all our neighbors, and taught you how to choose a ripe pineapple at the grocery store. I never stopped talking to you. You were my daughter, and I loved you as I love your sisters. We prayed for you all the time. Our prayers changed with the days. We never doubted that God could heal you. I know you know that. I know you felt that. But I still feel compelled to tell you that we believed, Audrey. And the fact that you are with Him as

I type these words *does not change our belief*. There is not a single moment that passes when I question His will for your life.

I will never forget the day you were born. Nobody who was a part of it will either. April 7 was one of the best days of my life. You made me brave, Audrey girl. Your mommy used to be afraid of the hospital, afraid of the noises and the smell of medicine. My whole life I have been afraid. I wasn't afraid that day. I was peaceful. I was calm. I was in the presence of the Lord Himself more than any other time in my life. I listened as they told me about what would happen that day, and I nodded. I surrendered. I stopped worrying about me and I just fell into the arms of the Lord. He carried us all that day, didn't He?

At 4:31, I heard a nurse say, "She's out." Daddy said, "She's out?" and he peeked around to see them carrying you to a table nearby. I thought I heard you squeaking, and I asked if you were alive. Daddy looked at me and he nodded. "She's alive." I couldn't believe it. The doctors looked you over, and they listened to your heart. They cleaned you off a little bit, and then Daddy laid you right beside my head. You had one little eye opened, and you were trying to take it all in. I was too. I put my hands on your head and just started crying because you were so beautiful. I fell completely, head over heels in love with you the instant I met you. That's who you are, Audrey.

When we got back to the room, your Uncle Tom was already taking pictures. Do you know that he took about sixteen hundred that day? We rejoiced in telling everyone that you were alive. Your heart was moving slowly, and we knew that it was a matter of time before we would have to release you, but no one would have known that. For the rest of the day, people held you, touched you, talked to you, and prayed for you. And everybody smiled when they saw you. There weren't many tears because in a way we weren't sad. We were just too busy praising God for you to be sad.

Your daddy gave you a bath while I watched. He got all of your little tootsies clean, and I watched the water run down the back of your neck as he held you up. *Her first bath.*

One of my favorite moments was when they put you on the scale. You were much bigger than they thought you were ever going to be, and it felt like victory. "Three pounds, two ounces!" As soon as the announcement was made, the room broke out into cheers. Did you know that your daddy's birthday is March 2 (3/2)? Those are beautiful numbers to us, sweet girl, because they tell us that you were here. You had weight in this life.

Your sisters were a little nervous when they came, but as they looked you over, God showed them who you were. The peace that had filled the room for the entire day rested on them, and they began to laugh and to talk to you as they would any other new baby. They each held you carefully and kissed your sweet, clean skin. While they were all gathered around me on the bed, your nurse Candace came to listen to your heart. I asked her to be sensitive because of the girls, and after listening for a few minutes, she told me quietly that you were gone. The girls never knew that they had been present for that moment, and I thank God that He took you that way. There was never anything but peace. We sang over you as God welcomed you into heaven.

I cry for you often. I miss the smell of your skin and your perfect little nose. My arms ache from emptiness. I tell your daddy all the time that I just want to hold you again. I cannot see to write these words because my eyes overflow with the tears of a mother who has been asked to give her daughter away. I knew I would love you when I met you. I knew you would become a part of me. What I didn't know was that instead of feeling like it was a brief encounter, I feel like the world stood still. He somehow gave us an entire lifetime of memories in such a short time. I didn't feel like I lost a baby; I felt like I said good-bye to someone I had always known, who had been my daughter for years and years. Even now, as I write, it seems impossible that you were only with us for two and a half hours. *Thank You, Lord, for giving us all the time we could have asked for with her.* The clock was insignificant. We knew you deeply, a lifetime's worth.

Audrey, you have no idea how you have impacted those around you. Did you see all of the nurses who cried when they came to see me? Did you hear the nurse manager tell me that since you had been born, the name of the Lord had been spoken repeatedly at their station in a way it never had? That you, my love, had brought them together? Did you know that the people who came to your birth who knew nothing of your story talked about the "amazing peace" that inexplicably filled the room? Do you know that radio stations all over the country announced that your mommy was going into surgery while people drove home to their families? Do you know they asked for prayer as you entered the world, that strangers dropped to their knees on your behalf? Do you know how many people have met Jesus because of you? There is more than I can fit here, Audrey. More than I can fit anywhere. You are the greatest miracle I have ever been a part of, and I want you to know how incredibly proud I am to have been chosen to be your mommy. I promise you that I will never stop being your voice here on Earth. I will tell everyone about the little girl who came in a three-pound body to change hearts. I will always miss you, Audrey; there will never be a day where you are not a part of us. I want you to know that you changed me, honey. You made Mommy so brave because of how much I loved you. I am so proud to have a scar to remember where you once were.

Thank you, my sweet, sweet girl.

Today we are going to sit as a family, and we are going to take the Band-Aids off the bunny that we have carried for months. We are going to tell your sisters about the way Jesus has healed you, that you don't need those anymore because you are well. You are perfect. *Thank You, Lord.*

As I have been writing, the rain is pounding on my window. It is what many would call a dark and ugly day, with no sign of sunshine. Because of you, Audrey, it is not that way to me any more. It is an answer to prayer.

Jesus, You have brought us the rain, and we praise You for it. We lift up the God that made us strong enough to love our little girl the way she deserved to be loved. And we trust that You will continue to use her as a vessel of Your goodness, of Your faithfulness. Lord, You have shown me that when this life is empty, You will fill. You have walked with us in a way we could never have imagined. What seemed like a cross to bear has now taken the shape of a great blessing, which we are honored to have been a part of. Thank You, Lord. You are the light of our lives, now and forever.

Audrey, there is much more to say. I rest in knowing that you already know it before it has left our lips. We love you.

Sweetest baby girl.

Do you know you changed the world?

Mommy

In the months that have passed since we lost our Audrey, I have learned that grief is a dance. I do it rather clumsily much of the time, but as it turns out, I am in good company. Others who have lost children have shared the inability to separate the sorrow from the joy in life. I find that they are inextricably woven, never to be pulled fully from each other in this life. I am reminded of this delicate dance as I think upon the Savior whose blood mingled with our freedom. I am an injured dancer, and yet one who wants her life to bring glory to the one who allowed sorrow and joy to dance at all.

Sorrowful, yet always rejoicing. (2 Cor. 6:10)

Sorrow was beautiful, but her beauty was the beauty of the moonlight shining through the leafy branches of the trees in the wood, and making little pools of silver here and there in the soft green moss below.

When Sorrow sang, her notes were like the low sweet call of the nightingale, and in her eyes was the unexpectant gaze of one who has ceased to look for coming gladness. She could weep in tender sympathy with those who weep, but to rejoice with those who rejoice was unknown to her.

Joy was beautiful, too, but his was the radiant beauty of the summer morning. His eyes still held the glad laughter of childhood, and his hair had the glint of the sunshine's kiss. When Joy sang his voice soared upward as the lark's, and his step was the step of a conqueror who has never known defeat. He could rejoice with all who rejoice, but to weep with those who weep was unknown to him.

"But we can never be united," said Sorrow wistfully.

"No, never." And Joy's eyes shadowed as he spoke. "*My* path lies through the sunlit meadows, the sweetest roses bloom for my gathering, and the blackbirds and thrushes await my coming to pour forth their most joyous lays."

"*My* path," said Sorrow, turning slowly away, "leads through the darkening woods; with moonflowers only shall my hands be filled. Yet the sweetest of all earth songs—the love song of the night—shall be mine; farewell, Joy, farewell."

Even as she spoke they became conscious of a form standing beside them; dimly seen, but of kingly Presence, and a great and holy awe stole over them as they sank on their knees before Him.

"I see Him as the King of Joy," whispered Sorrow, "for on His head are many crowns, and the nailprints in His hands and feet are the scars of a great victory. Before Him all my sorrow is melting away into deathless love and gladness, and I give myself to Him forever."

"Nay, Sorrow," said Joy softly, "but I see Him as the King of Sorrow, and the crown on His head is a crown of thorns, and the nailprints in His hands and feet are the scars of great agony. I too, give myself to Him forever, for sorrow with Him must be sweeter than any joy I have ever known."

"Then we are *one* in Him," they cried in gladness, "for none but He could unite Joy and Sorrow."

Hand in hand they passed out into the world to follow Him through storm and sunshine, in the bleakness of winter cold and the warmth of summer gladness, as sorrowful yet always rejoicing.[1]

I won't say that I don't still struggle with Audrey's death or that my thoughts don't ever drift into the land of "what if," but for the most part I am at peace with what the Lord has done. It hasn't been an easy road, and I know it will continue to challenge me for the rest of my days, but I am grateful that I can breathe again.

Where are you now?

Are you in the midst of it? Just on the other side? Wondering how your trial will end? We are all somewhere on the fringe or in the middle of a crisis, so I want to take a moment to share with you my most heartfelt prayer for you. Our Lord is bigger than any of the trials He asks us to walk through, yet I also recognize the hurt that threatens to steal our joy at any moment. It is a decision we must make, many times even in a day, to choose to believe that our Father is good. That sentence may be hard for you to read depending on where you are because we don't understand many of the ways the Lord works on our behalf.

Let me sit beside you for a moment, and imagine my arm wrapped in yours as I look into your face and tell you that I understand your hurt. I am not belittling your pain, nor do I want you to feel that you are weak or un-Christian because you hurt so much. Have you abandoned hope? Do you feel like there isn't a way out from where you are?

Sit here with me as long as you like and know that I am praying as I type these words. I am asking Jesus to bring you peace where you have none, and rest where you need to be still. I am asking Him to be near to you, as near as breath. I am asking the Lord to bless you with the most unexpected sense of expectation, believing against all odds that you have not been forgotten.

Before you close this book, let's sit together in prayer, bowing our heads to the One who raises the dead and restores faith where it has been shaken.

Will you allow me to do that?

Lord Jesus,

This is my prayer for myself and for all others who are walking in the shadow of loss. I long to glorify You with the words of my mouth and the meditation of my heart (Ps. 19). Please make Your presence known in the hearts of the hopeless, and as they read these words, I ask You to fill them with the peace that defies sorrow. May we each learn how to walk in full confidence of what You have planned for our lives and rest in that as the only truth.

I pray they will believe in You as the One who walked alongside Lazarus and the One who walks with us now.

You are mightier than death, Jesus, and I pray that my offering on Your behalf will bring You honor and joy.

We miss them, Lord.

We trust You to love them well, every day strengthening us to press on without them.

In Your name and only Yours, Amen.

If only my anguish could be weighed
and all my misery be placed on the scales!
It would surely outweigh the sand of the seas—
Job 6:2–3

Though he slay me, yet will I hope in him.
Job 13:15

---

1. Mrs. Charles E. Cowman, *Streams in the Desert* (Grand Rapids, MI: Zondervan, 1999), 316–18.

Chapter 16
My Jesus

*I want you to know that I sympathize deeply with
your trials. I present you before the Lord with all my
heart. I pray that as you are called to take part in the
sufferings of Jesus Christ, you will also take part in
His patience and submission.*

*The Lord is always near you as you seek His will
simply and sincerely. He will support you and
comfort you in times of trouble. Bring to Him
a calm and confident trust.*
—Jeanne Guyon

I would feel that I had done a great disservice to my readers if
I didn't include an invitation to love the Lord who walked with
me then and walks with me now and forevermore. If you have read
these words, and they have made you curious about what great
love has brought me here, I want to encourage you to seek counsel
in a local church to find out more about the Lord Jesus Christ.
Without Him there would be no words on the pages you have read,

nor would there even have been a story to begin with. He is the light that conquers darkness, and He wants to do the same in your life if He hasn't already.

If you feel ready to take that step of faith, the Bible tells us that we must confess with our mouths that Jesus is Lord. Bow before Him, believing that He is the One and only Son of God and that He came to Earth to rescue sinners with His love, perfect life, and sacrifice. To pay the penalty of our sin, He was crucified on a cross. Three days later, in fulfillment of the Scriptures, He rose from the grave and is now seated at the right hand of the Father. He has done this so that you might believe and put your life in His hands, being forgiven for all your sins and shortcomings, pressing into the great, invisible God who has every hair on your head counted and every breath determined.

When you have professed these things to Him, trusting in His perfection, you are invited to an eternity with Him in heaven, where there will be no more hurt, sorrow, regret, or suffering.

There we will see His face and His glory.

And I, for one, cannot wait to run to Him.

If this is a decision you are ready to make, and my Audrey had anything to do with your choice, I would be honored to know. Please contact my publisher so that we can pray and celebrate your new life.

I am profoundly grateful for the chance to share the gospel with you and blessed to know that my sweet daughter still speaks here.

And one day, in the blink of an eye, I will tell her so myself.

With much love and appreciation,

Angie

Angie Smith

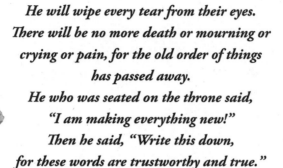

My eyes have grown dim with grief;
my whole frame is but a shadow.
Job 17:7

He will wipe every tear from their eyes.
There will be no more death or mourning or
crying or pain, for the old order of things
has passed away.
He who was seated on the throne said,
"I am making everything new!"
Then he said, "Write this down,
for these words are trustworthy and true."
Revelation 21:4–5

From Audrey's Daddy

Writing throughout my pregnancy and in the time since we lost Audrey has been such a blessing to me, but I've also prayed that it would be used by the Lord to encourage others going through similar circumstances. Men and women experience grief differently and often face different challenges in coping with the loss of a baby. Todd and I have realized this in our own experience and know it to be true with others as well. It's our prayer that the following reflections from Todd will help those facing a situation similar to what we faced with Audrey to understand your spouse more fully and for those around you to know how to minister to you as a couple more completely.

I was driving on the interstate one sunny December afternoon when I got a call from our nurse practitioner. She informed me that Audrey's test came back positive for Down syndrome. Since this particular test often had a high instance of false positives, Audrey had a 1 out of 120 chance of actually having the disorder. Yet I still worried about whether she would be the one out of 120 to have it. I was really worried. How would it affect our girls? How would it change our lives? Would I be a good father to a special-needs child? Why had God allowed this? Angie had prayed that if God was going to give a Down syndrome baby to anyone that He would give one to us. She has her master's degree in developmental psychology and specialized in helping kids with learning disabilities.

I prayed repeatedly that God would not give us a baby with Down syndrome. As we went in for our eighteen-week ultrasound, I had knots in my stomach. How were we going to deal with this? I tried to be brave, but I was so scared. I tried to act like I was fine with whatever God created, but inside I was anxious. In ten minutes everything changed. Audrey didn't have Down syndrome. She had kidney failure, an enlarged heart, and very small lungs. She had conditions that were incompatible with life. She wasn't going to live. It's interesting how your perspective can change when circumstances reveal themselves. I entered that building asking that Audrey not have Down syndrome and left begging God, "Please, just let it be Down syndrome."

The evening of April 6 I tried not to think about what was coming the next day. At the same time I tried to prepare myself for what was going to happen. I tried to rehearse the next day several times in my head, but there was no way to truly prepare. There is no way to plan for the birth of your child who you know is not going to survive. When Audrey was first diagnosed, we were told she would experience pain. We were told she would be incredibly disjointed. She would probably have multiple fractures and have a flat nose. All of these predicted deformities stemmed from the fact that she had little amniotic fluid to protect her. We decided that we would wait to see how she looked before we had our other three daughters come to the hospital. One of the most distinctive memories I have before she was born was waiting by the nurse's station on the top floor where Angie's C-section was to take place. The nurses took Angie into the operating room to prep her for the surgery while I waited for what seemed like forever but was actually about twenty minutes. My heart was beating fast, and I was breathing really heavy. I was so nervous and so scared. I knew in a few minutes I was going to see my daughter and just kept praying for God to give us strength. The doctors had said she would most likely gasp for breath and that she would live for a couple minutes at the most. She probably wouldn't make a sound, and she wouldn't move.

What would it be like to see my baby struggling to breathe and as a father be powerless to do anything about it?

They finally called me into the room. I remember seeing Angie lying down. She smiled when I got near her. She was so brave. Rather then risk Audrey's dying an immediate death by having a regular delivery, she offered her body to be C-sectioned for the chance to have a few precious minutes with her daughter. We held hands as I sat behind her, then the doctor notified everyone that they were starting. After several minutes they said, "She's out." I saw the nurse carrying her but didn't get a good glance at my Audrey until I stood over her while the nurse was cleaning her. She had beautiful red hair; she looked like our daughter Ellie when she was born. Most importantly she cried, and I saw her move! Those were two gifts I wasn't expecting. I expected a limp little baby girl, and God allowed me to see life in her. I brought her over to Angie, and we held her. She was so beautiful. She was wonderful. We told her how much we loved her and everything else we could think of to say. Angie finally said, "Baby, you don't have to stay. You can go home now." With those words we wept. We wept uncontrollably.

April 7 was the most peaceful day I have ever experienced. It was so joyful. We showed Audrey off to the world. The day wasn't one of, "Feel sorry for us." It was, "Here is our daughter. Look at her. Isn't she beautiful!" All her sisters got to hold her while she was still alive. We were hoping for a couple minutes with her. We were given two and a half hours with her! It was far too little but more than we had ever expected. Her passing was peaceful. The nurse checked her heart rate and nodded to Angie. Angie nodded back and smiled as she looked at her three older girls doting on their little sister. It was a beautiful day.

Angie and I grieved differently. For Angie it was a constant process from the time of Audrey's diagnosis, to the time of her passing, to now; for me it comes in cycles. Angie was constantly reminded of Audrey and was so connected with her because she was carrying her. She was always mourning for her. The grieving process has not been the same for me. I think that has been very difficult for Angie because it sometimes seemed as if I didn't love Audrey the way Angie did. It hurt her because I didn't grieve as intensely as she did. I think sometimes she felt alone. I was frustrated and angry with myself because I didn't grieve like she did. I felt guilty and in turn angry. I was very defensive.

It has always been difficult for me to connect completely with any of my daughters until they were born. It's not that way for every dad, but it was for me. Once I could see them, touch them, and hold them, then they were mine. I cannot express in words how much I adore and love my daughters. They are my greatest contribution to this world. I live for my family; however, it has always been difficult for me to connect with my children the way I wanted to when they were in the womb. I have always felt guilty about that but have never been able to change it.

Whereas so many nights Angie was heartbroken, I would be OK and was able to move forward. I went into survival mode. Part of me distanced myself from my daughter because I knew I was going to lose her. Part of me didn't want to deal with the whole thing. It is so overwhelming. You know every day you are one step closer to losing your child. Your family is hurting, and you are bearing burdens you don't know how you're going to overcome. I was also taking care of my wife and three girls, which was in itself overwhelming. The fear of not knowing what to expect was exhausting. Trying to distance myself was a coping mechanism that I'm still dealing with today.

Honestly I don't think I know how to grieve fully. I don't say that so you will feel sorry for me. I say it because I believe it's true. I think I wanted to avoid the pain, too. I didn't want to dig that deep. I didn't have the deep connection to Audrey that Angie did.

The grieving process would hit me suddenly. It has never been consistent or predictable. I remember one time being half asleep several days before we delivered Audrey, and I just started crying uncontrollably while I rested my head on Angie's belly. Recently I was leaving the grocery store, and I saw a father lifting his daughter as she pointed to the sky. You could see his delight as his little girl looked up in amazement. Audrey would have been the same age as the little girl, and the scene hit me so hard. One of our neighbors has a daughter whose due date was the same as Audrey's. I had forgotten that until one time while playing outside with the kids I saw the little girl sitting straight up in a little wagon. Suddenly I remembered they were the same age, and I became numb.

For fathers like me, the thing to remember is, there is no certain way to grieve. We all do it differently, and you don't need to feel guilty because you cry less. It doesn't mean you don't love your child. It's just how you deal with it. It is important that you *do* deal with it. I didn't deal with it the way I should have. Don't try to be tough, or have all the answers, or act like it's not affecting you. Please don't harden your heart to safeguard yourself from the child you are losing. I continue to grieve in my own way. It may come several times a week, or it may be several times a month; but when it hits, it hits hard. I'm more private in my grief and usually don't share about it. It is personal to me as I deal with the loss of my daughter.

If I could change anything, I think I would have spent much more time with Angie and Audrey. I remember the nights the three of us shared when everyone was asleep. I wish I had talked to Audrey more. I wish I had sung to her more. I wish I had journaled about what was happening. I wish I had been more sensitive to Angie. Many days I was overwhelmed and emotionally exhausted. Many times I wanted to do what I wanted to do instead of listening to what Angie needed.

Men, if there is one thing you need to listen to, it's this. If you are in a situation similar to what we faced losing Audrey and your wife asks you to choose what she needs over what you think is best, go with her. Even if it requires you to make difficult choices, listen to her. Angie asked me to do some big things. It wasn't that one of us was right and the other was wrong. Both of us were right, but we could only choose one. I chose to go with my plan; only after other people gave me counsel did I change my mind. That really put a gap between Angie and me. I listened to them but not to her. My intentions were good, but my wife needed to know she could count on me when she asked. Because your wife is carrying your precious child, you need to listen to her. It's different if what she is suggesting is not good for your family, but if the request is something you can do, no matter how difficult, go with her. It will draw you closer and save a lot of heartache later.

I remember reading a blog right after we got pregnant with Audrey, several months before we found out about her condition. This precious couple was where we were going to be even though I didn't know it yet. They knew they were going to lose their baby, and when they said they were going to praise God no matter the outcome, it made a huge impression on me. They made a decision that they were going to give God the glory no matter what He decided to do. Whether He healed her or took her, they were going to praise His name because they wanted their oldest daughter to know that they trusted Him. He is good. If He is good, then we need to praise Him no matter what comes our way, even when it doesn't make sense. Even when we come away not having answers. As a man it is so important that as you lead, you have one foot on Earth and one in heaven. I wasn't always successful at doing this.

Lean on other men. Don't run away from God. I understand the anger and the hurt, but you cannot do this on your own. Pray for God's help, for His wisdom, for Him to give you faith and hope, even when it feels pointless and hollow. Listen to your wife. Don't become an island. Don't get so quiet you won't talk about what's going on. Tell her how you feel. Ask God to give you compassion you never thought possible and patience as you take care of your family. There are going to be many days where your wife can't get out of bed. You are going to have to go to work and take care of her and your other children. You will have to be Mom and Dad to them. You can't do that on your own. You need time with God, you need time in prayer, you need other men you trust to support you and encourage you.

Be honest. You don't have it all together, and you don't have to act like you do. Give yourself, your spouse, and your children permission to grieve, to be angry, and to doubt. Protect your wife. There may be friends or other people you know that may not be good for her to be around during this season. Don't be afraid to say no—to turn people away, who may have great intentions but you know aren't right for you to be around right now. Don't be afraid to be the bad guy. You must provide a safe place for your wife and children to have space and to be themselves. Getting your wife though the pregnancy is more important than making friends feel comfortable. Your marriage is more important. Your kids knowing that you are a rock (even when inside you feel like you are crumbling), that you are a safe place, and that you will protect them is more important than someone's feelings, even if it's a dear friend.

Finally, if you are running from God, run to Him. Stay close to Him as you lead your family. You can be angry with Him the whole time, but go to Him. I believe God would prefer we yell and scream at Him but be in constant communication with Him than be silent and turn our backs on Him. This is a horrible situation, but it is one where you can see God make you into the man you need to be.

When we found out about Audrey's condition, we didn't hold back. She was our daughter, and we were going to make the most of the fourteen weeks we still had with her. We made her a part of our lives and in doing so brought our three other daughters into this experience. She is their sister. They knew right away that she had a *boo-boo* and that she was going to be with Jesus. They didn't fully understand, but we made them part of the journey. When they asked questions we didn't have answers to, and there were many, we would just say, "Honey, I don't know." It's OK to admit you don't.

One thing we did was take advantage of the moments we had. The girls wanted to show her Cinderella's castle, so we took her to Disney World. We took her to dances, movies, the theater, and the ballet. She was our daughter, and we were going to make the most of each second. We wrote a song for her, and when we recorded it, Angie had the headphones on her belly so Audrey could hear it. She kicked as Aunt Amy sang the lyrics. I sang to her, and Angie told her about everything she could think of to say. The girls would tell her stories, and we would read her stories. We have a lifetime of memories in those weeks because we chose to live and experience life with Audrey. If you are in a situation similar to ours, I encourage you to make those memories. Don't hold back. If you have other kids, let them be a part of it. They need to experience and grieve and love your baby just as much as you do. You would be amazed at what two- and four-year-olds can handle. We shared and experienced life with Audrey!

What do you say when someone you know is carrying a baby who is dying? One of the best words of advice I can give is to listen and say little. You don't have to say anything. Don't overspiritualize it. If there is a burning in your heart to share something, and it's not led by your own agenda, then share. When we lost Audrey, the last thing I wanted to hear was, "But you know, God's in control." Or, "Think of how He's going to be glorified through this." I know these things are true, but I don't want to hear someone say such things in the midst of losing my daughter. "Look at all the lives that have come to Him through Audrey's loss." I'm aware of that, and I'm grateful because it gives weight to her life, but to be perfectly honest, I would rather He use some other means to save them and give me my daughter back. These sayings are well intended, but they don't do anything to bring comfort to someone who has lost a child.

Please don't ever say, "Well, you have three other girls, right?" Having other children will never make up for the loss of Audrey. All my children are unique. I love them equally but differently. They are each a different face of God to me.

Just keep it simple. Have empathy. Simple words like, "I am so sorry for you, and I will be praying for you," are enough. It's horrible. It's devastating. We will never be the same. It will never be fixed in this life. We are completely powerless to do anything. There are no answers.

This doesn't mean you can't be encouraging, or you can't smile, but let people grieve. Sometimes it feels as though grieving is a sign of spiritual weakness, or that when we are grieving we have to tag it with, "But I know God is in control." Death is awful. It hurts you to your core. Don't sugarcoat death. It is what it is. Be there for them. Sit with them. Make meals for them. Go to their house and clean it for them. Go in with some people and pay for them to go on a vacation and get away for a while. Be gracious enough to let them bare their soul and not be judged for how they feel. You can minister so much by being present and saying little.

I have always believed that an infant goes to heaven. When a mother miscarries or terminates the pregnancy, I believe there is a soul that goes to be with God. However, when we found out about Audrey's condition, I couldn't remember why I believed Audrey would go to heaven. What did the Bible reveal?

The following verses were probably the most comforting Scriptures I read from the time we found out to the time we buried Audrey.

> *David noticed that his servants were whispering among*
> *themselves and he realized the child was dead. "Is the*
> *child dead?" he asked. "Yes," they replied, "he is dead."*

Then David got up from the ground. After he had washed, put on lotions and changed his clothes, he went into the house of the LORD and worshiped. Then he went into his own house, and at his request they served him food, and he ate. His servants asked him, "Why are you acting this way? While the child was still alive, you fasted and wept, but now that the child is dead, you get up and eat!"

He answered, "While the child was still alive, I fasted and wept. I thought, 'Who knows? The LORD may be gracious to me and let the child live.' But now that he is dead, why should I fast? Can I bring him back again? I will go to him, but he will not return to me." (2 Sam. 12:19–23)

Knowing that David had been used by the Lord to pen so many Scriptures and was led by the Spirit of God, verse 23 really gave me assurance of Audrey's home. David's child would not be nonexistent or go to some unknown place. David would go to his child in heaven. I will go to Audrey someday.

I Will Carry You (Audrey's Song)
by Todd Smith, Angela Carole Smith, Christa Wells

There were photographs I
wanted to take
Things I wanted to show you
Sing sweet lullabies
Wipe your teary eyes
Who could love you like
this?

People say that I am brave
but I'm not
Truth is I'm barely hanging
on
But there's a greater story
Written long before me
Because He loves you like
this

So I will carry you
While your heart beats here
Long beyond the empty
cradle
Through the coming years
I will carry you
All my life
And I will praise the One
who's chosen me
To carry you

Such a short time
Such a long road
All this madness but I know
That the silence
Has brought me to His voice
And He says

I've shown her photographs
Of time beginning
Walked her through the
parted seas
Angel lullabies
No more teary eyes
Who could love her like
this?

So I will carry you
While your heart beats here
Long beyond the empty
cradle
Through the coming years
I will carry you
All your life
And I will praise the One
who's chosen me
To carry you

Helping Children Grieve

I was grateful for my educational background during and after Audrey's life. One of the things I am asked on a regular basis is how I approached helping my children understand the situation. People wonder what we shared with them and what we withheld. I answer this the same way I answer questions about the Bible and teaching my children about the Lord. I don't shy away from the truth; I tell them everything I can but on a level I feel they can understand and process.

If you have been through something tragic as a parent, you understand the desire to shield them from sorrow and keep them from being overwhelmed. The truth is, the more we try to hide things and gloss over things, the more insecure they will be. Of course, the degree to which they experience this depends on a child's age.

The twins were five when we lost Audrey while Kate was two. The twins' understanding was a bit more than Kate's, but they all sensed that something was wrong before we had a chance to explain it. The shift in our home's atmosphere was palpable, and children even younger than Kate can sense that. Infants who are living in the wake of loss do not understand death, but they understand that Mommy is sad or that Daddy seems to be distant.

They need to be held and comforted, reassured that you aren't abandoning them to your grief.

Toddlers have a better understanding of death, but they have trouble understanding the idea of finality. We saw this a lot with Kate. We felt like she understood Audrey was dead but not necessarily comprehending that this meant she wouldn't ever be back. I relate to this in my own way; when I imagine heaven, it's impossible to comprehend the scope of eternity. Surely it can't go on forever, right? That was the way Kate seemed to process it so we took many opportunities to talk to her about heaven and the fact that we wouldn't have a baby to put in a crib. She needed tangible facts and constant reassurance when she was confused. Don't underestimate the degree to which a toddler processes this type of crisis. On one occasion I happened to glance in the rearview mirror, and I saw Kate, perfectly quiet but with tears covering her little cheeks. I asked her what was wrong, and she held out her hands in front of her, cupped as if there was a baby in them.

"We don't get to hold her." She continued crying. I stopped the car and went to her and told her how much it hurt me to think about that too. I told her that sometimes I cried because I missed Audrey so much.

Abby and Ellie process things differently, but as a general rule they were typical preschoolers in that the world appeared black-and-white. Traffic lights are either red or green. It is the truth, or it is a lie. There is no gray. They are trying so hard to grab hold of "the rules of life" that they have a hard time digging around the areas that aren't that simple. While you don't want to overwhelm your child with details, do include them in the knowledge you have available. After appointments we sat with the girls and told them what we had seen and how we felt. We made it a point to make them feel like they could say anything they wanted to us, and that it was safe to ask questions. You may notice that open-ended questions can be difficult for such a young child to respond to. Instead of saying, "How are you feeling?" I would suggest, "It seems like you're kind of sad today. Do you want to tell me about it?" or, "How about we sit down and work a puzzle, and we can talk a little bit about what you're thinking about."

Children are much more likely to express difficult feelings when they are somewhat busy with something else. I have found that when I am playing with the girls, I can role-play the dolls and get them to open up much more than if I just ask point-blank questions. Art is also a great way to encourage kids to share feelings. All three of mine told me more with their crayons than they ever did with their mouths. Once I was able to see what they had drawn, I could talk to them about it in a way that helped them process what they were feeling. Oftentimes they aren't mature enough to put such complex emotions into words, but they can allude to them and that's an opportunity for you to dig deeper.

For example, one day Ellie drew a picture of a deflated balloon, and I asked her about it. She ran into the other room and brought out a red balloon that had popped. She explained to me that she knew we couldn't keep the balloon, so she wanted to have a picture of it so we wouldn't forget. I asked her if she felt the same way about Audrey, if pictures of her would make her remember better, and she nodded. We sat at the computer and browsed through photos of her sister while I assured her that we would never forget.

They often drew pictures of caskets or of our family with Audrey. It was their way of trying to make it concrete, so we readily accepted the opportunities we got to share what we believed. Don't water down the truth; but rather, modify the version you give to be at the appropriate age level. Trust your intuition about the way your children understand the situation and adjust accordingly. I know there were times that I thought I was doing things in a way that would be best, but I realized that I had either shared more than they could handle or less than they needed to feel safe.

I prayed constantly for the Lord to cover over my errors and bless them with peace when I did things wrong. There isn't a game plan for explaining such horrible things to young children, but rest assured Jesus is able to fill the gaps and smooth the bumps.

I have hardly ever heard parents say they feel like they shared too much with their children, but rather that they wish they had included them more. We made the decision to have our children hold Audrey because we knew that the mystery of not seeing her would be more confusing to them than the opportunity for us to share her together. Others know that this wouldn't be the right choice for their kids. Ultimately the Holy Spirit will guide you as you make these difficult decisions.

The one thing I will say about grieving in the presence of your children is that you should. Don't hide away and wear a perfect smile, pretending that everything is OK; because whether or not you say it, they know it isn't. Your children know the way you make their beds, the way you cut their sandwiches, the way you kiss them good-night. They know when you're sad, and the more you alienate them from your emotions, the more you tell them that they shouldn't grieve either. Tell them you're sad. Tell them you wish the child were still alive. Tell them that some-times at night you cry too because you don't understand why it had to happen. By being transparent, you will show your children that you can handle their feelings, and they will be much more likely to share their hearts with you.

School-aged children will probably ask more questions about the possibility of dying themselves. They realize that this enemy can now strike, and to them nobody is safe. Make sure you allow your child to express his/her feelings without dismissing them. It doesn't help to say, "Oh, don't worry about that. You aren't going to die anytime soon. You're going to live a long, happy life." I once heard a mother say that to her child, and it made me want to scream. I understand the desire to save your child from worry but not to the extreme that you are lying. Be careful with your words, and instead of promising things you cannot control, tell your child about your trust in the Lord to take care of these things. Don't make children feel like it's silly to worry about, but at the same time don't overwhelm them with details.

It is usually enough to say that while it's natural to worry about something we don't understand, we try not to dwell on it. Children are often comforted by the idea of heaven, but don't rely on that to make them feel total relief. They want what they are familiar with and what they know is here. Be sure to talk to them about what heaven will be like and to reassure them about your faith in eternity with Jesus Christ but know that like any other unfamiliar thing, this place doesn't fix the hurt. It doesn't fix it for me, and I believe in it. How much harder is it for a child to comprehend?

Try as hard as you can to keep your family's routines intact. Bath time, bedtime, dinnertime, and other markers of your routine are important opportunities to show your children that there are constants in what may feel like chaos. We thought about pulling Kate out of her preschool so that we could spend more time with her while things were really bad, but I am so glad that we decided not to do so. She thrived because in a sense things were like they had always been, and that gave her a feeling of normalcy that she needed.

The need to follow a normal routine also includes being consistent with discipline. Many times we want to go easy on our kids because we feel like they are acting out against the situation, but the reality is that they will feel more secure when they see that the boundary lines haven't shifted. That doesn't mean that there isn't grace for behaviors that arise, but you should confront the behavior immediately and make it known that house rules have not changed. Contrary to what your emotions may tell you, coddling a child and allowing him or her to get away with behaviors that previously wouldn't have been accepted is a warning sign that things are different. This is frightening for a child. It is preferable to try and keep things as similar as you can to the time before the loss.

If you're in a situation similar to what we faced looking toward Audrey's birth, make sure you prepare your kids for what they are going to see. Is it a hospital room? Will there be cords and machines? Will people be crying? What is a funeral? What happens at a burial? Try your best to sketch the scene for them so that they feel like it won't be a complete surprise. If there are things your children hold dear, like a blankie or a toy, make sure they have that item with them during these times. Abby, Ellie, and Kate were shocked to see one of their favorite toys propped up in a chair at Audrey's burial service. We set him there right before it started, and they sat and told him all about the baby and why we were there.

The more you tell them, the more likely they will volunteer questions for you. We explained to our girls that Audrey was going to die, and that when she did, she wouldn't look any different right away but that her spirit would go and be with the Lord. We told them that while this was going to be terribly sad for us, it wasn't something we needed to fear because nothing was going to happen at that moment that we could see with our eyes. In fact, when she was declared dead, the girls nodded in acceptance. They knew this was something they were going to have to deal with because we had done our best to explain it beforehand.

I am well aware that many people do not have the opportunity to prepare their children, or themselves for that matter, for the death of a child. If this is the case for you, first and foremost, I want you to know that I am praying for you as I write these words. I am praying for the wisdom that only the Lord can give you and for the strength you need to grieve well. It is no easy task, even with months to prepare, and I know that the suddenness of death is such a different situation than what I went through.

I want to acknowledge your hurt and also the way that some of this is not possible for you. After my nephew died, I watched the way Greg and Nicol progressed, and it was very different than it was for me. It was thrust upon them with no warning and no time to formulate a plan for the way they would explain things to their daughter. They did an amazing job of telling things to her in a way that was simple and yet direct. She is one of the sweetest, brightest, most loving children I have ever met, and being around her reminds me of how well they loved her through it all.

After we lost Audrey, we gave the girls necklaces with tiny hearts on them to remember their sister. Tangible mementos are wonderful reminders for your child; possibly a photo album, a rattle, a blanket, or a toy that reminds him or her of the sibling that died are wonderful ways to remind them that the child was real.

Spend one-on-one time with each of your kids. They tend to respond differently when there isn't anyone else there. You will probably find that they open up more easily than when no one else is there. Ellie did this a lot, and I know it's because she never wanted to add to the sadness of her sisters. She felt like her job was to hold everything together, and she needed a place where she could speak freely. Take your child to get a milkshake or go for a long walk and focus wholly on him or her. This will create a sense of security, as well as a feeling of validity and importance. Children who have lost a sibling need constant reminders that they are just as special as the child who is gone.

It's common for children to have bad dreams after such a loss and to be fearful of sleeping. Talk through the fears with them, and make sure you are spending time praying with them before bedtime, reading Scripture that will bring them peace (I love Psalm 91). Teach them how to pray when they feel afraid, even giving them Scriptures to memorize for moments when you aren't there. Here are a few I really love:

1. "The LORD is my shepherd, I shall not be in want." (Ps. 23:1)
2. "The LORD is my light and my salvation—whom shall I fear? The LORD is the stronghold of my life—of whom shall I be afraid?" (Ps. 27:1)
3. "The LORD is my helper; I will not be afraid." (Heb.13:6)
4. "So do not fear; for I am with you; do not be dismayed, for I am your God. I will strengthen you and help you." (Isa. 41:10)
5. "Be strong, do not fear; your God will come." (Isa. 35:4)

Children are easily able to shift gears and may go from crying one minute to laughing hysterically at a movie. Don't be concerned about this; children's emotions are sporadic at this age, and it doesn't signify a problem. I believe God allows children a special grace not only to take breaks from grieving but also to have a sense of the Lord that we may not. My children have told me countless stories of the way they thought they saw an angel in their rooms or that Jesus had whispered to them. I feel like I have been jaded by knowledge, while a child's grief has a sweet innocence. It can be a source of tremendous healing for parents to see the peace their children settle into and to know that the Lord wants the same for them.

If your child is acting out in ways you deem exceptionally different or more persistent and intense than before, address their behavior immediately. If children have issues with rage and aggression or crippling anxiety, seek help from a child psychologist or counselor. You are the only one who knows your child well enough to detect these types of changes, but I want to encourage you to act on your instincts and get help if it's needed.

In talking to women from previous generations, I have sensed how much they carry the weight of the unknown. Some women who lost a sibling tell me their mothers never spoke of it, but they felt like they couldn't live up to whoever the child would have been. Many blame themselves for the loss and carry the guilt of being a survivor. Tell your children that yes, you are sad, and yes, you miss the child that has died, but also that you are so grateful that you have him or her.

I met a woman a year or so ago who told me that when her mother died, she found a little box of pictures and baby items. After speaking to relatives, she found out she had a brother who died in his infancy. She was never told and said that the fact that her mother had kept this from her was so devastating that she could hardly bear it. She cried openly as she told me, and I saw the longing of a woman who wanted to be trusted with the truth. I know, as does she, that her mother's intention was to protect her, but that wasn't actually the effect. I am grateful that we approach miscarriage, stillborn, and infant death differently now and that there are so many resources for women who are trying to figure out how to navigate this path with their families.

Bibliography

Alcorn, Randy. *Heaven.* Chicago: Tyndale, 2004.

Beasley-Murray. George R. *John: Word Biblical Commentary Vol. 36.* Nashville: Thomas Nelson, 1999.

Bernstein, Judith R. *When the Bough Breaks: Forever after the Death of a Son or Daughter.* Kansas City, MO: McMeel Publishing, 1998.

Cowman, Mrs. Charles E. *Streams in the Desert.* Grand Rapids: Zondervan, 1999.

Davis, Deborah L. *Empty Cradle, Broken Heart: Surviving the Death of Your Baby.* Golden, CO: Fulcrum Publishing, 1996.

Faber, Rebecca. *A Mother's Grief Observed.* Chicago: Tyndale, 1997.

Floyd, Gregory. *A Grief Unveiled: One Father's Journey Through the Death of a Child.* Brewster, MA: Paraclete Press, 1999.

Guthrie, Nancy. *Holding On to Hope: A Pathway through Suffering to the Heart of God.* Chicago: Tyndale, 2006.

Guthrie, Nancy and David. *When Your Family's Lost a Loved One: Finding Hope Together.* Colorado Springs: Focus on the Family Publications, 2008.

Guyon, Jeanne. *Experiencing the Depths of Jesus Christ.* Goleta, CA: Christian Books, 1980.

Kidd, Sue Monk. *When the Heart Waits: Spiritual Direction for Life's Sacred Questions*. New York: Harper Collins, 1990.

Lewis, C. S. *A Grief Observed*. New York: HarperOne, 2001.

MacArthur, John. *Safe in the Arms of God: Truth from Heaven about the Death of a Child*. Nashville: Thomas Nelson, 2003.

Nouwen, Henri. *Turn My Mourning into Dancing: Finding Hope in Hard Times*. Nashville: Thomas Nelson, 2001.

Sittser, Jerry. *A Grace Disguised: How the Soul Grows Through Loss*. Grand Rapids: Zondervan, 1999.

Ten Boom, Corrie. *The Hiding Place*. New York: Bantam Books, 1971.

Wolterstorff, Nicholas. *Lament for a Son*. Grand Rapids: Eerdmans, 1987.

Wright, H. Norman. *Experiencing Grief*. Nashville: B&H Publishing Group, 2004.

Wunnenberg, Kathe. *Grieving the Child I Never Knew*. Grand Rapids: Zondervan, 2001.

Helpful Resources

Now I Lay Me Down to Sleep: Organization that has photographers all over the country trained to photograph babies expected to die. (www.nilmdts.com)

Be Not Afraid: A great Web site with stories of babies that lived despite an adverse diagnosis. This is a good resource for those who have received a potentially fatal diagnosis and are considering termination. (www.benotafraid.net)

Griefshare: An organization that has meetings around the U.S. as well as several other countries. It is a wonderful site for book recommendations and working through your grief, with a search option to find a group that meets near you. (www.griefshare.org)

Lisa Leonard Jewelry: Beautiful jewelry site with a necklace called "The Audrey" made for those who want to commemorate their lost child. Jewelry can be personalized and makes a special gift for someone who has lost a child. (www.lisaleonard online.com)

Engraved Tiles: The sweet owner of this site sent me a tile commemorating my precious Audrey, and I fell in love with her work. Her gift meant the world to me, and I think it makes a wonderful gift for grieving parents. (www.engravedeuniques.com)

Baby Be Blessed: Gorgeous, personalized dolls including Scripture patches and the child's name.
(www.babybeblessed.com)

Acknowledgments

I want to start by thanking my incredible Lord, the only One who should receive glory for this book. He has been more to me than I can write, and my prayer is that He is glorified by the one He chose to hold the pen.

To my Toddy—I love you more than I thought I could. You are one of the best men I have ever known, and I am grateful to be the woman you chose. I can't wait for all the tomorrows that wait for us. Thank you for your unending encouragement as I wrote this book and for doing more loads of laundry and dishes than anyone I know as I sat upstairs writing. You are a blessing to me, baby. You are a blessing to all of us.

For Ellie, Abby, and Sarah-Kate—There is no way you could know how much I love you or how many times I have asked myself what I did to deserve to be your mommy. You are my most precious gifts, and I humbly accept the role of guiding you into the women God intends for you to be. It is one of the greatest honors of my life to love you all. Thank you for understanding that Mommy needed to write these words for your sister, and thank you for praying for me while I did.

For my mom and dad—Thank you for believing in me when I didn't. I am so grateful for who you are and what you have sacrificed with joy in order to parent me so well. I love you both so much.

Jenn—I love you so much and have treasured watching you grow into an amazing woman and a spectacular mom. You are such a blessing to me, and I am honored to call you a sister and a friend.

Audra—You know there aren't words. You know it all, friend. Thank you for being my rock for so many years and for being a woman of God, eager to honor Jesus with your life. Shawn, Amelia, and Aliza are so blessed to have you. Thank you for teaching me through your life and your words how to be better and for loving me through it all so well. You are everything I could have asked for in a "Diana." A+

Jess—You have been one of the most selfless, beautiful examples of a friend that anyone could imagine. You never failed me. You were always ready with a prayer, with an idea, with a solution, with a shoulder to cry on. I love you (and Matthew and Elias!).

Dan—I'm so glad I inherited you from your life with Todd! You are one of my best friends, and you have walked every bit of this road with us. You are a pillar of strength and a beautiful example of friendship, and I want you to know how much we all love and appreciate you.

For Todd's family—you walked with us in the deepest valleys and loved us back to safety. Thank you. Greg and Nicol (and Summer), I continue to grieve with you, knowing that your hearts will never fully heal in this life. Luke was a beautiful, precious baby, and I thank the Lord I had a chance to know him. Thank you for allowing me to share your story along with mine and for being such great friends to us throughout all of it.

For Jennifer Lyell—You know that you are so much more than an editor, and I thank the Lord for your grace, passion, and dedication to telling Audrey's story. Thank you for caring more about her than the page count and the font. Thank you for your infectious love of the Lord and overwhelming desire to serve Him with your life. How do I thank you for helping tell the story of my daughter? You are a gift to me, and I am more grateful than you will ever know that the Lord blessed me with your friendship.